WEAVING IT TOGETHER

3

Milada Broukal

Glendale Community College

Heinle & Heinle Publishers
A Division of Wadsworth, Inc.
Boston, Massachusetts 02116 U.S.A.

The publication of *Weaving It Together 3* was directed by members of the Newbury House Publishing Team at Heinle & Heinle:

Erik Gundersen, **Editorial Director**
Kristin Thalheimer, **Production Editor**

Also participating in the publication of this program were:

Publisher: Stanley J. Galek
Editorial Production Manager: Elizabeth Holthaus
Project Manager: Hockett Editorial Service
Manufacturing Coordinator: Mary Beth Lynch
Photo Coordinator: Martha Leibs-Heckly
Assistant Editor: Karen Hazar
Associate Marketing Manager: Donna Hamilton
Production Assistant: Maryellen Eschmann
Interior Designer: Winston • Ford Visual Communications
Illustrator: James Edwards
Cover Illustrator: Lisa Houck
Cover Designer: Judy Ziegler

Photo Credits (page numbers are given in boldface):
1—Philip Jon Bailey, Stock, Boston; **23**—Patrick Watson, The Image Works; **24**—John Elk, Stock, Boston; Chapter **34**—Randall Human, Stock, Boston; **43**—George Bellerose, Stock, Boston; **44**—Ron Alexander, Stock, Boston; Chapter **57**—W. Hill, Jr., The Image Works; **69**—Mark Richards, PhotoEdit; **70**—The Bettmann Archive; **80**—Gordon Parks; **91**—Scala/Art Resource, Arcimboldo, "The Fall"; **92**—John Elk, Stock, Boston (chili peppers); George Bellerose, Stock, Boston (fishing boat); **104**—Alan Oddie, PhotoEdit (Japanese tea); Ulrike Welsch (English tea); **127**—Jon Burbank, The Image Works; **140**—Gontier, The Image Works; Chapter **151**—Jean-Claude Lejeune, Stock, Boston

• •

Heinle & Heinle Publishers is a division of Wadsworth, Inc.

Manufactured in the United States of America

Library of Congress Cataloging-in-Publication Data

Broukal, Milada.
   Weaving it together 3
      1. English language—Textbooks for foreign speakers.
I. Title.
PE1128.B715   1993   428.2′4   92–43932
ISBN 0-8384-4221-8 (v. 1)
ISBN 0-8384-3977-2 (v. 2)
ISBN 0-8384-4222-6 (v. 3)

CONTENTS

Unit 1: Symbols

Unit 2: Customs

Unit 3: Mind and Body

Unit 4: People

Unit 5: Food

10 Tea, Anyone?   104

Unit 6: Language

11 Our Changing Language   116

12 English Around the World   127

Unit 7: Technology

TO THE TEACHER

Rationale

Weaving It Together, Book 3, is the third in a three-book series that integrates reading and writing skills for students of English as a second or foreign language. The complete program includes the following:

> **Book 1 . . . Beginning level**

> **Book 2 . . . High beginning level**

> **Book 3 . . . Intermediate level**

The central premise of *Weaving It Together* is that reading and writing are interwoven and inextricable skills. Good readers write well; good writers read well. With this premise in mind, *Weaving It Together* has been developed to meet the following objectives:

1. To combine reading and writing through a comprehensive, systematic, and engaging process designed to effectively integrate the two.
2. To provide academically bound students with serious and engaging multicultural content.
3. To promote individualized and cooperative learning within the moderate- to large-sized class.

Over the past few years, a number of noted researchers in the field of second language acquisition have written about the serious need to effectively integrate reading and writing instruction in both classroom practice and materials development. *Weaving It Together* is, in many ways, a response to this need.

Barbara Kroll, for example, talks of teaching students to read like writers and write like readers (1993). She notes: "It is only when a writer is able to cast himself or herself in the role of a reader of the text under preparation that he or she is able to anticipate the reader's needs by writing into the text what he or she expects or wants the reader to take out from the text." Through its systematic approach to integrating reading and writing, *Weaving It Together* teaches ESL and EFL students to understand the kinds of interconnections between reading and writing that they need to make in order to achieve academic success.

Linda Lonon Blanton's research focuses on the need for second language students to develop authority, conviction, and certainty in their writing. She believes that students develop strong writing skills in concert with good reading skills. Blanton writes: "My experience tells me that empowerment, or achieving this certainty and authority, can be achieved only through performance—through the act of speaking and writing about texts, through developing individual responses to texts." (1992)

For Blanton, as for Kroll and others, both reading and writing must be treated as composing processes. Effective writing instruction must be integrally linked with effective reading instruction. This notion is at the heart of *Weaving It Together*.

Organization of the Text

Weaving It Together, Book 3, contains seven thematically organized units, each of which includes two interrelated chapters. Each chapter begins with a reading, moves on to a set of activities designed to develop critical reading skills, and culminates with a series of interactive writing exercises.

Each chapter contains the following sequence of activities:

1. **Pre-Reading questions:** Each chapter is introduced with a page of photographs or drawings accompanied by a set of discussion questions. The purpose of the pre-reading questions is to prepare students for the reading by activating their background knowledge and encouraging them to call on and share their experiences.

2. **Reading:** Each reading is a high-interest, nonfiction passage related to the theme of the unit. Selected topics include The Many Faces of Medicine, Our Changing Language, and The Global Telephone.

3. **Vocabulary:** The vocabulary in bold type in each reading passage is practiced in the vocabulary exercise that follows the passage. The vocabulary items introduced and practiced provide a useful source for students when they are writing their own essays on the same theme.

4. **Comprehension:** There are three types of comprehension exercises. The first, *Looking for the Main Ideas*, concentrates on a general understanding of the reading. This exercise may be done after a first silent reading of the text. Students can reread the text to check answers. The second comprehension exercise, *Looking for Details*, concentrates on developing skimming and scanning skills. The third comprehension exercise, *Making Inferences and Drawing Conclusions*, develops the skill of inferring meaning from what is not directly stated in the passage.

5. **Discussion:** Students may work in small or large groups and interact with each other to discuss questions that arise from the reading. These questions ask students to relate their experiences to what they have learned from the reading. The questions in the *Discussion* section can provide information on one of the topics to be written on in the *Writing Practice* section.

6. **Model essay:** This essay in each unit is written by an international student whose writing skills are slightly more advanced than those of the writers who will use *Weaving It Together, Book 3*. The essay follows the general rhetorical form of North American academic prose, and provides a natural preparation for the more discrete points taught in the organizing section.

7. **Organizing** With each of the fourteen readings, a different aspect of essay organization is developed. These aspects include essay organization, structure, transitions, and rhetorical devices the student will use to develop his/her own essay. Exercises following the points taught reinforce the organizational techniques introduced.

8. **Pre-writing:** Brainstorming and clustering techniques are presented and practiced in this section of the text. These help students activate their background knowledge before they start to write.

9. **Developing an outline:** Using the ideas they have generated in the pre-writing section, students put together an outline for their writing. This outline acts as a "framework" for the work ahead.

10. **Writing a rough draft:** A rough draft of the essay is written. *Weaving It Together* encourages students to write several rough drafts, since writing is an ongoing process.

11. **Revising your draft using the checklist:** Students can work on their own or with a partner to check their essays, and make any necessary alterations. Teachers are encouraged to add any further points they consider important to the checklist provided.

12. **Editing your essay:** In this section, students are encouraged to work with a partner or their teacher to correct spelling, punctuation, vocabulary, and grammar.

13. **Writing your final copy:** Students prepare the final version of the essay.

Journal Writing

In addition to the projects and exercises in the book, I strongly recommend that students be instructed to keep a journal in which they correspond with you. The purpose of this journal is for them to tell you how they feel about the class each day. It gives them an opportunity to tell you what they like, what they dislike, what they understand, and what they don't understand. By having students explain what they have learned in the class, you can discover whether or not they understand the concepts taught.

Journal writing is effective for two major reasons. First, since this type of writing focuses on fluency and personal expression, students always have something to write about. Second, journal writing can also be used to identify language concerns and troublespots that need further review. In its finest form, journal writing can become an active dialogue between teacher and student that permits you both to learn more about your students' lives and to individualize their language instruction.

References

Blanton, Linda Lonon (1992). "Reading, Writing, and Authority: Issues in Developmental ESL." *College ESL,* 2, 11–19.

Kroll, Barbara (1993). "Teaching Writing *Is* Teaching Reading: Training the New Teacher of ESL Composition," in *Reading in the Composition Classroom* (Heinle & Heinle Publishers, Boston), 61–81.

TO THE STUDENT

This book will teach you to read and write in English. You will study readings on selected themes and learn strategies for writing a good essay on those themes. In the process, you will be exposed to the writings and ideas of others, as well as to ways of expressing your own ideas so that you can work toward writing an essay of four or five paragraphs in good English.

It is important for you to know that writing well in English may be quite different from writing well in your native language. Good Chinese or Arabic writing is different from good English writing. Not only are the styles different, but the organization is different too. Good Spanish organization is different from good English organization.

The processes of reading and writing are closely interconnected. Therefore, in this text we are weaving reading and writing together. I hope that the readings in this text will stimulate your interest in writing, and that *Weaving It Together* will make writing in English much easier for you.

Milada Broukal

ACKNOWLEDGMENTS

I would like to express my gratitude to the following individuals who reviewed *Weaving It Together, Book 1,* and who offered many ideas and suggestions: Cheryl Benz, Miami-Dade Community College; P. Charles Brown, Concordia University, Montreal; Barbara Rigby-Acosta, El Paso Community College; Greg Conner, Orange Coast College.

My very special thanks to my wonderful editor Erik Gundersen for his insights and encouragement throughout this work. I am also grateful to Karen Hazar and the rest of the Heinle & Heinle team who worked on this project.

I would like to take this opportunity to thank my mother and father for their unremitting love and support throughout my projects.

UNIT 1

Symbols

Chapter 1: Color Me Pink

PRE-READING QUESTIONS

Discuss these questions with your classmates or teacher.

1 Imagine yourself as the man in the picture. How would you feel if the room were all blue?

2 How would you feel if the room were all red?

3 How would you feel if the room were all black?

4 What color would you like this room to be?

Reading: Color Me Pink

Red, white, pink, purple—what is your favorite color? We are all sensitive to color. There are some colors we like a lot and some we don't like at all. Some colors **soothe** us, others excite us, some make us happy, and others make us sad. People are affected by color more than they realize because color is tied to all aspects of our lives.

Experts in colorgenics, the study of the language of color, believe that the colors we wear say a lot about us. Do you know why you select a shirt or dress of a certain color when you look through your clothes in the morning? Colorgenics experts say that we **subconsciously** choose to wear certain colors in order to communicate our desires, emotions, and needs.

Colorgenics experts claim that our clothes send messages to others about our mood, personality, and desires. For these experts, pink expresses the peace and **contentment** of the wearer. People who often wear pink are supposed to be warm and understanding. The message is that you would like to share your peace and happiness with others. Red garments, on the other hand, indicate a high level of physical energy. People who wear red like to take life at a fast **pace**. Brown is the color of wealth and it shows a need for independence and material security. Wearers of green have a love of nature and enjoy peaceful moments. They often like to be left alone with their thoughts.

Although colorgenics may be a recent area of study, associating colors with emotions is not new. Colors have always been used to describe not only our feelings, but also our physical health and attitudes. "Red with rage" describes anger; "in the pink" means to be in good health; "feeling blue" is a sad way to feel; and "green with envy" indicates a jealous **attitude**.

Color is used symbolically in all cultures and it plays an important role in ceremonies and festivities. Yellow is a symbol of luck in Peru and it can be seen just about everywhere during New Year celebrations—in flowers, clothing, and decorations. Some Peruvians say, "The more yellow you have around you, the luckier you will be in the new year." Yellow is also an important color to the Vietnamese, who use it at weddings and also on their flag, where it represents courage, victory, and sacrifice. In many cultures, white symbolizes purity, which is why brides often wear white wedding gowns. Black, on the other hand, symbolizes death, and it is often the color people wear to funerals.

According to colorgenics experts, colors not only are a mirror of ourselves, but they have an effect on us as well. Blue is calming, while red is **stimulating** and exciting. It's no **coincidence** that racing cars are often painted red. Yellow is a happy color that makes us feel good about life. Pink awakens love and kindness.

Some experts are so convinced that colors have a strong effect on us that they believe colors can be used to heal. They say that by concentrating our thoughts on certain colors, we can cause energy to go to the parts of the body that need treatment. White light is said to be cleansing, and it can balance the body's entire system. Yellow stimulates the mind and creates a positive attitude, so it can help against depression. Green, which has a calming and restful effect, is supposed to be good for heart conditions. Books are now available that teach people how to heal with color. These books provide long lists of **ailments** and the colors that can heal them.

Some psychologists and physicians also use color to help them treat patients with emotional and psychological problems. By giving them what is called the Luscher color test, in which people select the colors they like and dislike, doctors can learn many things about a patient's personality.

In conclusion, the study of color can help us to understand ourselves and to improve our lives. It offers an alternative way to heal the body and spirit, and it can help us understand what others are trying to communicate. We can then respond to their needs and achieve a new level of understanding.

··

VOCABULARY

Complete each definition with one of the following words.

soothe	coincidence	subconsciously
attitude	ailments	pace
stimulating		contentment

1. People who are sick have

   _____.

2. To _____ someone is to

   comfort the person and make the person feel better.

3. Something that excites us and makes us active is

   _____.

4. To do something _____ is to

   act without actively knowing it.

5. Things happen by _____ if

   they appear to be connected in some way but really are not.

6. _____ is the feeling or

   emotion you have toward something.

7. To be happy and at ease is to feel

   _____.

8. _____ is the speed at which

   we do things.

COMPREHENSION

A. Looking for the Main Ideas

Circle the letter of the correct answer.

1. Learning about color can help us to

   _____.

   a. express ourselves more clearly

   b. control our desires

   c. understand ourselves and others

2. Colors _____.

   a. have similar meanings around the world

   b. are not often used in a symbolic way

   c. say something about our personality

3. Some experts believe _____.

   a. colors can be used to heal

   b. associating colors with emotions is something new

   c. most colors have a calming effect on us

B. Looking for Details

Scan the passage quickly to find the answers to these questions. Write complete sentences.

1. What to colorgenics experts say about a person who likes to wear pink?
2. What does white symbolize in many cultures?
3. What is yellow a symbol of in Peru?
4. According to colorgenics experts, how does red make us feel?
5. According to colorgenics experts, how does blue make us feel?
6. According to some experts, green is a color for healing. What part of the body do they think it is good for?
7. What is the name of the test used by some psychologists to help them treat their patients?

C. Making Inferences and Drawing Conclusions

The answers to these questions are not directly stated in the passage. Write complete answers.

1. Why might it be good for a decorator to study colorgenics?
2. Why is color an important part of ceremonies and festivities?
3. Why might the Luscher color test help a psychologist treat a patient?
4. How might learning about color be useful in our lives?

DISCUSSION

Discuss these questions with your classmates.

1. What colors are you wearing today? Do you think they are a reflection of your feelings?
2. Look at the colors your classmates are wearing. Do you think the colors they are wearing match their personalities?
3. Do some colors make you feel better than others?
4. What colors are symbolic in your culture?

WRITING

ORGANIZING

A paragraph is a basic unit of organization in writing a group of sentences that develop one main idea.

There are three parts to a paragraph:

1. A topic sentence
2. Supporting sentences
3. A concluding sentence

1. THE TOPIC SENTENCE

The **topic sentence** is the most important sentence in the paragraph. It is the main idea of the paragraph. The topic sentence controls and limits the ideas that can be discussed in a paragraph.

The **topic sentence** has two parts: the **topic** and the **controlling idea**.

The **topic** is the subject of the paragraph.

Example:
The color yellow is the color of mental activity.

       Topic: The color yellow

The **controlling idea** limits or controls your topic to one aspect that you want to write about.

Examples:

             Topic   Controlling idea
              ↓   ↓
Brown is the color of <u>material security</u>.

or

             Topic   Controlling idea
              ↓   ↓
Brown shows <u>a desire for stability</u>.

A topic can have more than one controlling idea. You could write one paragraph about the color brown indicating material security and another on the desire for stability.

Exercise 1

Circle the topic and underline the controlling idea in each of these topic sentences.

1. The colors we wear change our emotions.
2. People who wear orange like to communicate with others.
3. People who wear red clothes want to have fun.
4. Shoes give us lots of information about the person wearing them.
5. Patterns on clothing give us clues to the mood of the wearer.
6. People who wear yellow are often creative.
7. Turquoise is good for people who have decisions to make.
8. People who wear green often like the outdoors.

2. SUPPORTING SENTENCES

Supporting sentences develop the topic sentence. They give the reader reasons, examples, and more facts about the topic sentence. They must all be related to the topic sentence.

Exercise 2

Look at the underlined topic sentences. In each case, one of the sentences below it does not support the topic sentence. Circle the letter of your answer.

1. Colors are often divided into two groups, warm and cold.
   a. The warm colors are red, pink, yellow, and orange.
   b. These colors are associated with activity and energy.
   c. Violet is the color of royalty and is often worn by political and religious leaders.
   d. The cold colors—blue, purple, violet, and brown—are calm and mysterious.

2. Socks and stockings give us clues to a person's inner personality.
   a. Socks and stockings are available in more colors now than ever before.
   b. Red socks show that the wearer has lots of energy that he/she needs to let go of.
   c. Wearers of white socks and stockings are often hiding their true feelings.

     d. Green socks are worn when a person feels the need for rest and relaxation.

  3. The Luscher color test is made up of eight colors that have been carefully chosen for their meanings.

     a. Dr. Max Luscher, the inventor of the test, was born in Basel, Switzerland, in 1923.

     b. Each of the eight colors has the same meaning and importance the world over.

     c. The colors in the test are gray, blue, green, red, yellow, violet, brown, and black.

  4. Colors are symbolic and have many different meanings to people around the world.

     a. In America, red, white, and blue, the colors of the flag, symbolize patriotism.

     b. Green is a sign of birth and new life to the Irish.

     c. Blue looks good on people with blue eyes.

     d. Some colors represent male and female, such as pink and blue.

3. THE CONCLUDING SENTENCE

The last sentence of your paragraph is called the **concluding sentence**. This sentence signals the end of the paragraph.

The concluding sentence is similar to the topic sentence. They are both general sentences. The concluding sentence can be written in two ways:

  1. State the topic sentence in *different* words.

or

  2. Summarize the main points in the paragraph.

Begin a concluding sentence with one of these phrases:

     In conclusion, . . .

or

     In summary, . . .

Write a topic sentence for each of these paragraphs.

1. Topic Sentence: _____

   _____

       If your favorite color is white, you are probably very moral and sometimes have old-fashioned ideas about romance. People who like red, on the other hand, want excitement, variety, and change, and are often more interested in passion than true love. Pink lovers are warm and understanding people who believe in loyalty and make good mates. Those who like the color blue are emotional and romantic and need lots of attention from their partners.

2. Topic Sentence: _____

   _____

       Violet is a color that affects the bones in the body and can be used to heal the pain of arthritis. Gold helps awaken a body's own healing energy. Blue clears the mind, and aqua is cooling and can ease fever.

3. Topic Sentence: _____

   _____

       To make a color wheel, draw a circle and divide it into twelve equal parts. Then color in each section, starting with red. Notice how you feel as you color each section. You may feel more drawn to some colors than to others. Some colors make you feel better than others. Think about which colors are good for your health.

Chapter 2: And the Lucky Number Is . . .

PRE-READING QUESTIONS

Discuss these questions with your classmates or teacher.

 1 What are the superstitions connected with these symbols?

2 How superstitious are you?

3 What do you think is your lucky number?

Reading: And the Lucky Number Is . . . . .

Do you believe that seven is a lucky number or that things happen in sets of three? If so, your ideas are as old as Pythagoras, a Greek philosopher of the sixth century B.C. Pythagoras believed that certain numbers and their multiples had mystical power. For centuries, people have given importance to numbers and developed superstitions about them. Many of these superstitions have been passed on through the generations and still exist today.

Many of the superstitions surrounding numbers have a basis in science and nature. For example, early astrologers believed that seven planets governed the universe and therefore the lives of human beings. A seventh child was thought to have special gifts. Human life was divided into seven ages. Every seventh year was believed to bring great change. If a person's date of birth could be divided by seven, that person's life would be lucky. For the ancient Babylonians, three was a lucky number because it symbolized birth, life, and death. Some people still believe that a dream repeated three times comes true.

Numbers don't have the same meaning in all cultures. Five is considered a most holy and lucky number in Egypt. But in Ghana, the Ashanti people consider five to be an unlucky number. To give someone five of anything is to wish the person evil. The ancient Greeks and Egyptians thought the number four was a perfect number symbolizing unity, **endurance**, and balance. However, the Chinese consider the number four to be unlucky because it sounds like the word for death.

The number that seems to be almost universally considered unlucky is thirteen. No other number has had such a bad reputation for so long. The ancient Romans regarded it as a symbol of death, destruction, and **misfortune**. One of the earliest written stories about the number thirteen appears in Norwegian mythology. This story tells about a feast at Valhalla to which twelve gods were invited. Loki, the god of evil, came uninvited, raising the number to thirteen. In the struggle to throw out Loki, Balder, the favorite of the gods, was killed.

There are many superstitions regarding the number thirteen. For example, in Britain it's considered a bad **omen** for thirteen people to sit at a table. Some say that the person who rises first will meet with misfortune, even death, within a year. Others say it's the last person to rise. Some British people think it's unlucky to have thirteen people in a room, especially for the person closest to the door. The thirteenth day of the month isn't considered a good day on which to begin any new **enterprise**, including marriage, or to set out on a journey. Many people believe that

Friday the thirteenth is the unluckiest day in the year. This belief is so widespread that there are horror movies called "Friday the Thirteenth."

Some people will go to great lengths to avoid the number thirteen. Hotel owners do not usually **assign** the number thirteen to a room, preferring to label it 12A or 14 instead. The French never issue the house address 13, while in Italy the number thirteen is **omitted** from the national lottery. Airlines have no thirteenth row on their planes, and office and apartment buildings rarely have a thirteenth floor.

From ancient civilizations to modern societies, the belief in the magic of numbers has **persisted** in spite of the advances in science and technology. There is nothing quite as stubborn as superstition. Even as we approach the twenty-first century, people still believe in bad luck and omens. In the future, people may work in space stations or travel the universe in starships, but there probably won't be a "Starbase 13" or a rocket liftoff on Friday the thirteenth. A seventh voyage will be a good one, and the third time around will still be lucky.

VOCABULARY

What are the meanings of the underlined words? Circle the letter of each correct answer.

1. Four was considered to be a perfect number symbolizing unity, <u>endurance</u>, and balance.
    a. lasting
    b. equality
    c. independence

2. The Romans regarded thirteen as a symbol of death, destruction, and <u>misfortune</u>.
    a. bad luck
    b. opportunity
    c. injury

3. It's considered a bad <u>omen</u> for thirteen people to sit at a table.
    a. promise
    b. sign
    c. action

4. The thirteenth is not considered a good day on which to begin any new underline{enterprise}.

    a. building

    b. project

    c. journey

5. Hotel owners will not usually underline{assign} the number thirteen to a room.

    a. transfer

    b. choose

    c. give

6. In Italy, the number thirteen is underline{omitted} from the lottery.

    a. left out

    b. repeated

    c. added

7. The belief in the magic of numbers has underline{persisted}.

    a. gone away

    b. become greater

    c. continued

COMPREHENSION

A. Looking for the Main Ideas

Circle the letter of the correct answer.

1. Throughout the ages, people have

    _____.

    a. written stories about numbers

    b. given meaning and importance to numbers

    c. considered five a lucky number

2. Numbers _____.

    a. have different meanings in different cultures

    b. have the same meaning everywhere

    c. didn't have much meaning in ancient times

3. The number thirteen _____.

    a. is omitted from the lottery in every country

    b. was a good number for the ancient Romans

    c. is considered unlucky almost everywhere

B. Looking for Details

Scan the passage quickly to find the answers to these questions. Write complete sentences.

1. What was special about a seventh child?
2. What do some interpreters of dreams believe about a dream repeated three times?
3. What year was believed to bring change in a person's life?
4. Why was three a lucky number to the ancient Babylonians?
5. Where is five considered a holy and lucky number?
6. What did the number four symbolize to the ancient Greeks?
7. Where did one of the earliest written stories about the number thirteen appear?
8. For what is the thirteenth day of the month considered unlucky?
9. What do hotel owners do to avoid assigning the number thirteen to a room?

C. Making Inferences and Drawing Conclusions

The answers to these questions are not directly stated in the passage. Write complete sentences.

1. What influence did Pythagoras have on the beliefs we have about numbers?
2. Why might a seventh child be thought of as special?
3. Why would a hotelier avoid assigning the number thirteen to a room?
4. What effect have science and technology had on our belief in the power of numbers?

DISCUSSION

Discuss these questions with your classmates.

1. What superstitions do you have in your country?
2. What are the lucky and unlucky numbers in your country?
3. Describe an object that is a symbol. Where and how is it used?

Writing an Essay

An essay is a piece of writing that is several paragraphs long. An essay is about one topic, just like a paragraph. Since its topic is broad, the essay is divided into paragraphs, one for each major point. To tie all the parts together, an introduction is added to the beginning and a conclusion to the end.

An essay has three parts:

1. An **introduction**
2. A **body** (one, two, or more paragraphs)
3. A **conclusion**

The **introduction** has two parts: **general statements** and a **thesis statement**. The general statements give the reader background information about the topic of the essay. These statements should get the reader interested in the topic. The **thesis statement** introduces the main idea of the essay. It is just like a topic sentence in a paragraph. It states the main topic and tells what will be said in the body paragraphs. The thesis is usually the last sentence of the introduction.

The **body** of the essay consists of one or more paragraphs. Each of these paragraphs has a topic sentence, supporting sentences, and sometimes a concluding sentence. The body paragraphs support whatever is mentioned in the thesis statement. The body paragraphs are similar to the supporting points of a paragraph.

The **conclusion** is the last paragraph of the essay. It summarizes the main points discussed in the body or restates the thesis in different words. It also leaves the reader with a final comment or thought about the topic.

Transitions or **linking words** are used to connect the paragraphs. These are just like the transitions used in the paragraphs to connect ideas between sentences.

Look at the following diagram of an essay and note how it corresponds to the parts of a paragraph.

The Essay

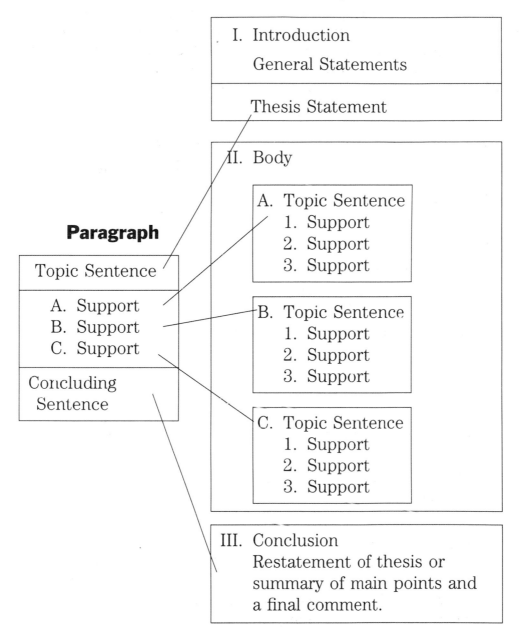

Paragraph

Topic Sentence
A. Support B. Support C. Support
Concluding Sentence

I. Introduction

General Statements

Thesis Statement

II. Body

A. Topic Sentence
   1. Support
   2. Support
   3. Support

B. Topic Sentence
   1. Support
   2. Support
   3. Support

C. Topic Sentence
   1. Support
   2. Support
   3. Support

III. Conclusion
Restatement of thesis or summary of main points and a final comment.

The Thesis Statement

The essay is controlled by one main idea. This main idea is called the thesis statement. The thesis statement is similar to the topic sentence in the paragraph, but it is broader and gives the controlling idea for the whole essay. Each of the topic sentences in the body paragraphs should relate to the thesis statement.

It is important to remember these points about a thesis statement.

1. The thesis statement should be a complete sentence.

2. The thesis statement should express an opinion, an idea, or a belief. The thesis statement should be something that you can argue about. It should not be a plain fact.

Example:

Not a thesis statement:
   Water consists of hydrogen and oxygen.
Thesis statement:
   The water in our homes may contain harmful chemicals.

3. The thesis statement should not be a detail or an example.

Example:

Not a thesis statement:
   In Hong Kong, number eight is lucky.
Thesis statement:
   There are many superstitious beliefs about even numbers around the world.

4. The thesis statement may state or list how it will support an opinion.

Example:

Thesis statement:
   Television has a bad influence on children for three main reasons.
Thesis statement:
   The choice of food we eat during our New Year's festival in India is influenced by tradition and religion.

Exercise 1

Read the following sentences. Some are thesis statements, some are details. Put check marks next to the thesis statement.

_____ 1. People have always been superstitious about cats.

_____ 2. In certain parts of Asia, people believed that they became cats when they died.

_____ 3. It was thought that to cut your nails on Sunday would bring you bad luck.

_____ 4. There are many superstitions that are similar in several countries around the world.

_____ 5. There is a superstition among sailors that says wearing earrings will save a sailor from drowning.

_____ 6. It is believed that our health and physical condition have an effect on our dreams.

_____ 7. It is said that to knock over the salt on a table is to meet trouble.

_____ 8. Throughout history, the luck of odd numbers has been a matter of superstitious belief.

_____ 9. Dreams of field, sea, country, and difficult roads and journeys are believed to be a sign of heart trouble.

_____ 10. Many superstitions can be traced to ancient civilizations.

Now read the following essay written by a student.

Superstitions in My Country

In the Middle East, especially Syria where I come from, people believe in some superstitions. Some of these superstitions are so strong that they are almost customs. These superstitions are about protecting against evil and bringing good luck. Two of the most popular superstitions are concerned with the evil eye and throwing water.

People believe that they must protect themselves from the evil eye of another person by putting turquoise beads in various places. A blue bead is pinned on newly born babies because babies are more vulnerable to an evil spirit and must be protected. Since houses must be protected too, a blue bead, usually with a horseshoe, is placed near the doorway for protection against someone with an evil eye. Also, if people have an item of special value like a car or sewing machine they must protect it with a blue bead.

Another popular superstition is throwing water, which is done at various times. When someone leaves on a trip, people throw water out of the window to wish them a good trip. This is so they will go and come back like water. Water is also thrown out when a funeral procession goes by the street, so that death will not come into their homes. The Armenians, who are Christians who live in Syria, throw water on each other on a special Saint's day in mid-July for fertility and prosperity.

In conclusion, certain superstitions have become rituals with the purpose of protecting and bringing good luck. Because people always want to be protected and have good luck, these age-old superstitions are as strong today as they were ages ago and probably will continue in the future.

Look at the student essay on the previous page and complete the following essay outline.

Essay Outline

I. Introduction
Thesis Statement: _____

_____

II. Body
A. Topic Sentence: _____

_____

    1. Support: _____

_____

    2. Support: _____

_____

    3. Support: _____

_____

B. Topic Sentence: _____

_____

    1. Support: _____

_____

    2. Support: _____

_____

    3. Support: _____

_____

III. Conclusion

DO YOU KNOW THESE SYMBOLS?

Do you know the answers to these questions about symbols? Circle the letter of the correct answer.

1. When the bride and bridegroom leave the church in Western countries, rice or confetti (strings of paper) is showered on them. Why is confetti used?
    a. Because paper is a symbol of life
    b. Because confetti is less dangerous to the face and eyes than rice
    c. Because rice is not found everywhere

2. What Japanese animal (worn as an amulet) is the symbol of abundance and riches?

    a. The fish

    b. The eagle

    c. The rabbit

3. In Burma, these animals are worn (as amulets) by children to protect them against the evil eye. In Italy, Greece, and Turkey, these animals carved in amber are symbols of good health. What are these animals?

    a. Dolphins

    b. Eagles

    c. Frogs

4. The wedding ring, a gold band that symbolizes never-ending love, is placed on the third finger of the left hand. Why is it placed on the third finger of the left hand?

    a. Because that finger has no other use

    b. Because it is believed that there is a nerve in that finger that connects to the heart

    c. Because that finger is a symbol of good health

5. The horseshoe is an ancient symbol of luck in the West. How is a horseshoe placed on the wall?

    a. It is placed with the ends pointing horizontally.

    b. It is placed with the ends pointing up.

    c. It is placed with the ends pointing down.

6. In the West, what does a ringing in one's right ear mean?

    a. It means you will get good news.

    b. It means you will get bad news.

    c. It means someone is saying bad things about you.

7. What color symbolizes love in Jewish traditions and also symbolizes the south for the Navajo Indians?

    a. Red

    b. Blue

    c. White

UNIT 2

Customs

Chapter 3: An American Holiday— Hawaiian Style

PRE-READING QUESTIONS

Discuss these questions with your classmates or teacher.

1 What is happening in the picture?

2 What do you know about Hawaii?

3 How do you think they might celebrate Thanksgiving?

Reading: An American Holiday—Hawaiian Style

Fireworks. Hot dogs. Bands marching down Main Street. These are the pictures that come to many people's minds when they think of U.S. holidays. But the United States is a vast country made up of people from many different cultures, and the celebration of holidays reflects this diversity.

In the Chinatown section of San Francisco, rice and snow peas are a part of many holiday meals. In New Mexico, one might encounter chili peppers, *pinatas*, and Mexican music on the Fourth of July. In Hawaii, one popular way to celebrate a holiday is with a feast, or *luau*, which has been a Hawaiian tradition for centuries.

Hawaii is the only state in the United States that was once an independent country with its own language and culture. Today, many Hawaiians continue to celebrate traditional Hawaiian holidays, such as Prince Kuhio Day, Kamchameha Day, and Aloha Week. In celebration of their Hawaiian ancestry, Islanders might dress in traditional clothes such as loose dresses called *muumuus* or colorful shirts. Around their necks they might wear *leis*, or rings of flowers.

Even when it comes to celebrating a traditional American holiday such as Thanksgiving, Hawaiians give it their own special flavor. They might place pumpkins on doorsteps and **paste** cardboard pilgrims on windows, but chances are there will also be a turkey or a pig roasting under the ground in an earth oven, or *imu*.

Cooking in an *imu* is an ancient Islands custom that requires much work and cooperation among family members. Preparations begin several days before Thanksgiving when the family goes down to the beach or to the mouth of a stream to fill sacks with smooth, rounded lava stones. They choose the stones carefully for their shape and size and for the presence of holes that will prevent the rocks from exploding when they are heated.

To prepare the *imu*, the men first dig a large hole in the shape of a bowl about three feet wide and two feet deep. They then **line** the bottom and sides of the hole with the lava rocks. Firewood is cut and **piled up**, ready for the holiday morning when a fire is lit inside the hole. As the fire gets bigger and hotter, more rocks are placed in the hole. Finally, the lava rocks get so hot that they glow red and white. The fire is then brushed aside and several of the hot rocks are placed inside the turkey or pig. The meat is then wrapped in the long, broad leaves of the *ti* plant and tied up tightly with wire.

Before the pig or turkey is placed in the *imu*, chopped pieces of banana plant are spread over the hot rocks. The white, juicy lining of this plant makes a lot of steam, but it can also cause a bitter taste, so *ti* leaves are layered over it. Finally, the pig or turkey is placed in the *imu*, along with sweet potatoes, pineapple, plantain, vegetables, and even fresh fish—all wrapped in *ti* leaves.

More hot rocks are spread over the **bundles** of food, then more *ti* leaves, a layer of wet sacks, and a canvas covering. Dirt is **shoveled** into the hole and **patted down** smoothly. Not a **trace** can be seen of either the meal or the earth oven in which it is cooking.

Three to four hours later, the dirt is shoveled away. The men dip their hands in cold water and then quickly remove the burned leaves and rocks, allowing delicious smells to **emerge** from the oven. The bundles of cooked food are taken out, uncovered, and placed on platters, ready for a different kind of Thanksgiving meal, cooked and served Hawaiian style.

VOCABULARY

Complete each definition with one of the following words.

line	piled up	patted down
trace	emerge	pasted
bundles	shovel	

1. A number of things one on top of the other are

   _____.

2. Something stuck to something else with paste is

   _____ to it.

3. A _____ is a sign that

   something existed in a certain place.

4. If something were _____, it

   would be tapped or hit gently to flatten or smooth it.

5. To cover the inside of something is to

   _____ it.

6. To _____ is to come into view.

7. When digging a hole in the ground, to lift and throw the dirt with a special tool is to _____.

8. _____ are groups of things fastened or tied together.

COMPREHENSION

A. Looking for the Main Ideas

Circle the letter of the correct answer.

1. American holidays _____.
    a. are not usually celebrated by the Hawaiians
    b. are not celebrated in the same way throughout the country
    c. are similar to ancient Islands customs

2. The Hawaiians celebrate Thanksgiving

    _____.

    a. at a different time of year than other Americans
    b. in the same way that they celebrate all their holidays
    c. with some typically American and some Hawaiian customs

3. The steps that are taken to prepare a Hawaiian Thanksgiving dinner _____.
    a. begin several days in advance of the holiday
    b. involve the women only
    c. have little to do with their native traditions

B. Looking for Details

Complete the following sentences.

1. A popular way to celebrate a holiday in Hawaii is with a

    _____.

2. The Hawaiians like to roast their pig or turkey in

    _____.

3. Before Thanksgiving, family members go down to the beach to

_____.

4. After the men dig a large hole, they

_____.

5. When the lava rocks are so hot that they glow, then

_____.

6. Three items that are placed in the oven with the pig or turkey are

_____,

_____, and

_____.

7. After the hot rocks are spread over the food,

_____,

_____, and

_____ are placed over the

rocks.

8. _____ hours after the oven is

covered, the dirt is shoveled away.

C. Making Inferences and Drawing Conclusions

The answers to these questions are not directly stated in the passage. Write complete sentences.

1. Why are American holidays celebrated differently in certain parts of the United States?
2. How is Hawaii different from the other states in the United States?
3. Why do Islanders dress in traditional clothes on holidays?
4. How are preparations for a Hawaiian Thanksgiving a family affair?
5. Why is dirt shoveled over the hole and patted down?

Discuss these questions with your classmates.

1. Describe a method of barbecuing in your country.

2. Describe a very old tradition that is still practiced during your holidays and festivals.

3. Are there certain tasks that men do and women do during a preparation for a special festival or occasion?

Read the following essay written by a student. Underline the thesis statement and the topic sentence in each of the body paragraphs.

The Dragon Boat Festival

The Dragon Boat Festival is another significant festival in Chinese traditional celebrations. The Dragon Boat Festival is celebrated on the fifth day of lunar May. This holiday is to commemorate the death of Chyu Yuan, a well-loved poet of the fourth century B.C. Chyu Yuan drowned himself to protest his king's despotic rule. The villagers respected him so much that they rowed their boats down the river and dropped *chung-tze*, rice dumplings, into the river to feed the fish, so the fish would not eat Chyu Yuan's body. To celebrate the Dragon Boat Festival, families do several things, like make chung-tze, hang the moxa herb, and watch the dragon boat race.

Before the Dragon Boat Festival, every family prepares chung-tze. This is a kind of rice dumpling filled with various things, such as bean curd, meat, mushroom, and shrimp, and then wrapped in bamboo leaves and steamed. The mother and the children all work together in preparing the chung-tze.

Then each family also has to buy moxa herb and hang it in a special location. The reason for this is that the moxa herb can get rid of the bad luck in the family atmosphere. Some people even use these herbs to wash sick babies for they believe that this special festival can bring some "transformation" in people's lives. Usually the father and the boys find a location to hang the moxa herb.

After preparing the chung-tze, each family goes to the river to watch the dragon boat races, which take place on this festival. The dragon boat symbolizes the story of Chyu-Yuan. It is a rowing boat team competition with about thirty people in each team. All the spectators cheer and shout enthusiastically. After the exciting race, both the competitors and the spectators usually eat many chung-tze.

The Dragon Boat Festival symbolizes the unique meanings of Chinese history and furthermore, the process of making the rice dumplings, the hanging of the moxa herb, and the boat race are a way of drawing all members of the family together again. Perhaps one day we will have a very different celebration, but so far I still like this holiday being celebrated in a traditional way.

ORGANIZING

Chronological Order

Chronological order means time order. In writing an essay, time order is often used to describe events over a period of time in a person's life or during a historical event. Time order can also be used to show how something works or the steps in a process.

In all kinds of chronological order or time order essays, you should use transition signals and time expressions to make the time sequence clear. The following are some time order words and phrases:

Some Time Order Words

> First, . . . (Second, third, etc)
> Next, . . . or The next step . . .
> Then, . . .
> Finally, . . . Last, . . .
> Before . . . /After . . .
> Meanwhile
> Three hours later . . .
> In the morning . . .
> At 6 o'clock

Look at the reading passage and underline the words that show time order in the preparation of the Thanksgiving dinner.

The Introduction

The introduction of an essay has two parts:

1. General statements
2. A thesis statement

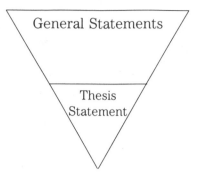

1. General Statements

The first statement of an introduction should be a general statement about the topic. The second sentence should be less general, the third sentence should be even less general, and so on until it leads to the thesis statement. The number of general statements you write in an introduction depends on how long your essay is. However, you should write at least two or three general statements in an introduction.

General Statements

- Introduce the topic of the essay
- Give background information on the topic

2. The Thesis Statement

The thesis statement is often the last sentence of the introduction. It is also the most important sentence in the introduction. It gives the specific topic and the controlling ideas for the whole essay. It may list the subtopics that will be discussed in the body paragraphs and may state the method of organization.

The Thesis Statement

- Is the last sentence of the introduction
- States the specific topic
- May state the subtopics
- May state the method of organization

The following are introductory paragraphs for essays describing a series of events on a special day. The sentences in these introductions are not in the correct order. Rewrite each introduction, beginning with the most general statement and ending with the thesis.

Introduction 1:

(1) Sometimes weddings are planned more than a year in advance because there are many events and procedures that must not be forgotten. (2) The traditional American wedding is formal and has many steps, each of which has a symbolic meaning. (3) Most people love their wedding day and remember it for the rest of their lives. (4) A great deal of preparation and expense go into planning a wedding.

Introduction 2:

(1) April Fool's Day is celebrated on the first of April in most countries. (2) If, like me, you don't know what day it is, you may be in for a surprise. (3) It is a day when people have a lot of fun. (4) People often play tricks on each other. (5) Last April Fool's Day is a day I will never forget because three very surprising things happened to me.

Introduction 3:

(1) The reason for the festivities is explained in stories handed down through generations. (2) Ga Homowo is a festival of Thanksgiving celebrated by the Ga people of Ghana. (3) They had the first festival after the harvest and it is now celebrated annually. (4) Unlike most annual festivals, Ga Homowo is made up of a series of events and celebrated within family groups. (5) These stories trace the origin of Ga Homowo to the first immigrants of the Ga tribe who landed on the shores of Ghana.

Introduction 4:

(1) It was on this day in 1776 that the original thirteen colonies declared their independence from England. (2) There are a series of events in which these people can participate. (3) Americans celebrate their day of independence on the fourth of July. (4) A new nation was born. (5) In celebration of that day, people get together with friends and family.

WRITING PRACTICE

Write an introduction with general statements and a thesis for an essay on the following topic.

Name an important occasion in your country. Describe how you prepare for it.

Chapter 4: Hop to It!

PRE-READING QUESTIONS

Discuss these questions with your classmates or teacher.

1 What is happening in the picture?

2 What other event with animals do you know about?

3 What do you think of people training animals for performance?

Reading: Hop to It!

"**H**e's good enough for one thing, I should judge—he can outjump any frog in Calaveras county," said Smiley in Mark Twain's famous short story "The Celebrated Jumping Frog of Calaveras County." This was the **inspiration** for the Calaveras County Jumping Frog Contest that has taken place since 1928 in the village of Angels Camp in Calaveras County, California. The first year, fifteen thousand people attended this unusual event, more than the entire population of Calaveras County at the time. The following year, the crowd doubled, and by 1931, the event was so popular that two additional jumping areas had to be added to **accommodate** entries from around the world. Today, more than fifty thousand spectators attend this event and the frog entries number one thousand.

Although the Calaveras Jumping Frog Contest has gained international attention, the majority of the competitors are still people from Calaveras County. Anyone who would like to enter goes to the registration table, fills out a form, and pays a **modest** entry fee. The fee includes the cost of renting a frog in case the entrant doesn't already own one. Many people who live in the area go out and catch their frogs the night before, so they are "fresh" and ready to go on the day of the contest.

After entering the contest, the competitors must decide who will be the "jockey." This is the person who places the frog on the **launching pad** and then encourages the frog to jump. The goal of the entrants and their "jockeys" is, first of all, to have fun; second, to win a prize; and third, to set a new world frog-jumping record.

The contest starts when the "jockey" positions his/her frog and then yells, screams, jumps up and down, puffs, blows, whistles, or does whatever else is necessary to **incite** the frog to jump. The one thing that is not allowed is any kind of physical contact with the frog. Each frog is given fifteen seconds to jump three times. Once a frog has made its three jumps, an official measures the distance from the center of the pad to the spot where the frog landed on its third jump. Naturally the winning frog is usually the one that jumped in the straightest line rather than zigzagged around. Some frogs **frustrate** their "jockeys" by jumping back toward the launching pad after a spectacular first or second jump.

Like any of nature's creations, frogs are **unpredictable**—that is, unless they have been to Bill Steed's famous Croaker College. Steed's "students" are given a 240-hour frog training course to teach them the **fundamentals** of frog jumping under pressure. At Croaker College, the frogs work out in a pool, lift tiny weights, do chin-ups and high dives, eat centipede soup and ladybug salad, and generally prepare for the big day. Do graduates of

Croaker College really win frog-jumping contests more often? That's a question Jim Steed prefers not to answer.

After the winners have been announced and the prizes given, the participants can take their frogs (or return their "rentals") and go home, or they can stay and enjoy the rest of the Calaveras County Fair. They can listen to country music, view craft displays, attend a horse race, watch a farm animal **auction,** and more. For those people who think nothing quite compares to the excitement of the jumping frogs, however, there is the **consolation** of knowing there is always next year.

VOCABULARY

What are the meanings of the underlined words? Circle the letter of the correct answer.

1. This is the underline{inspiration} for the Calaveras County Jumping Frog Contest.
    a. influence
    b. information
    c. description

2. Two jumping areas had to be added to underline{accommodate} the entries from around the world.
    a. invite
    b. announce
    c. provide for

3. Anyone who would like to enter pays a underline{modest} entry fee.
    a. small
    b. expensive
    c. formal

4. The "jockey" places the frog on the underline{launching pad}.
    a. winner's circle
    b. take-off point
    c. measuring place

5. The "jockey" does whatever is necessary to incite the frog to jump.
   a. excite
   b. calm
   c. demonstrate

6. Some frogs frustrate their "jockeys."
   a. upset
   b. satisfy
   c. anger

7. Frogs are unpredictable.
   a. experienced
   b. surprising
   c. native

8. At Croaker College, frogs are taught the fundamentals of jumping.
   a. possibilities
   b. basics
   c. origins

9. People can attend a farm animal auction at the fair.
   a. show
   b. contest
   c. sale

10. There is the consolation of knowing there's always next year.
    a. pressure
    b. benefit
    c. comfort

A. Looking for the Main Ideas

Circle the letter of the correct answer.

1. The Calaveras County Jumping Frog Contest

   _____.

   a. is an expensive but popular event

   b. is a formal international event

   c. is an unusual but popular event

2. The Jumping Frog Contest

   _____.

   a. is open to everyone, even those without frogs

   b. allows only graduates of Croaker College to participate

   c. allows only the people with frogs caught in the area to participate

3. The purpose of the contest is

   _____.

   a. to find the best frogs in the world

   b. for people to have a good time

   c. to bring people to Calaveras County

B. Looking for Details

Scan the passage quickly to find the answers to these questions. Write complete sentences.

1. Where did the idea for the Jumping Frog Contest come from?
2. How often does the Jumping Frog Contest take place?
3. Approximately how many people attend the Jumping Frog Contest today?
4. What does the entry fee include?
5. What can people do if they don't have a frog?
6. What does the "jockey" do?
7. How many jumps must the frog make before an official measures the distance?
8. List three things Bill Steed's students do in their training course.

C. Making Inferences and Drawing Conclusions

The answers to these questions are not directly stated in the passage. Write complete sentences.

1. Why is the Calaveras County Jumping Frog Contest so popular?
2. Why do you think there is only a modest entry fee?
3. Why would a "jockey" be frustrated if his/her frog jumped back to the launching pad?
4. Why are frogs unpredictable?

DISCUSSION

Discuss these questions with your classmates.

1. What special event that is not a holiday takes place in your country every year?
2. What customs in the United States or in other countries seem unusual to you?
3. Describe an event that requires special clothing or costumes.

WRITING

ORGANIZING

The Conclusion

The final paragraph of your essay is the **conclusion**. It tells the reader you have completed your essay. This is done either by summarizing the main points in the body of your essay or by rewriting the thesis statement using different words. Then you add a final comment or thought on the subject.

Begin your conclusion using a transition signal such as

> **In conclusion, . . .**
> **In summary, . . .**
> **To summarize, . . .**

The Conclusion

- Summary of the main points or restatement of the thesis in different words
  and
- A final comment or thought on the subject

Write conclusions for essays with the following introductions.
Example:

Introduction

On October 31, Americans celebrate Halloween. Halloween means "holy evening." This is the evening before the Christian holy day of All Saints Day. However, Halloween is older than Christianity. Before Christianity, people in Britain believed that the ghosts of the dead came back on this day, and so had rituals to scare the ghosts. Immigrants came from Europe to America and brought with them the custom of Halloween, as well as the many symbols and activities associated with this day.

Conclusion

In conclusion, Halloween as it is celebrated in the United States today still has many of the symbols and rituals brought over by the European immigrants. Although it is an old custom, it is a lot of fun. People will continue to celebrate Halloween for a long time to come.

Introduction 1:

Like other countries, Japan has its strict rules for table manners. These rules date back to the sixteenth century when the Ogasawara system of manners was developed. With the creation of this system, table manners reached an art form. These rules involve how the food is served, how the chopsticks are handled, and the order in which the foods are eaten.

Conclusion 1:

_____

_____

_____

_____

_____

Introduction 2:

Birthdays have been around for more than five thousand years. In every part of the world, they are celebrated in a slightly different way. One traditional American birthday celebration was brought over by the Europeans. The elements, such as a birthday song, a cake, candles, and gifts, are symbolic. In the United States, many birthday celebrations involve these elements.

Conclusion 2:

_____

_____

_____

_____

_____

Write an introduction and conclusion for an essay on the following
topic.
Describe a local custom or event in your country.

**DO YOU KNOW
THESE CUSTOMS?**

Circle T if the custom is true. Circle F if the custom is false.

1. In Scotland on New Year's Eve, most people eat haggis   T   F
   (stuffed sheep's intestine), turnips, and potatoes.

2. It is a custom for holy men and women in India to wear the   T   F
   color white.

3. In Turkey, whenever a person drinks Turkish coffee, he/she   T   F
   must turn the cup over on the saucer for good fortune.

4. In Mexico, it is a custom to shower the bride with paper   T   F
   money as she dances at the reception.

5. In Hawaii and Oceania, the New Year there, a festival called T   F
   makahki is celebrated in mid-October.

6. The custom of decorating Christmas trees at Christmas   T   F
   started in England in the 1700s.

UNIT 3

Mind and Body

Chapter 5: Bumps and Personalities

PRE-READING QUESTIONS

Discuss these questions with your classmates or teacher.

1. What do this person's eyes tell you?
2. How does a person's smile tell anything about that person?
3. Do people have different shapes of heads? What does a person's head shape tell you about the person?

Reading: Bumps and Personalities

Have you ever been afraid of or attracted to someone just because of the way the person looks? When you first meet someone, it is not unusual to react to his/her appearance. But these are first impressions, and most people assume that it takes time to find out what someone is really like. It is possible, however, that a person's appearance reveals more than we realize. According to some experts, a person's face, head, and body can **reveal** a great deal about personality.

Since ancient times, people have practiced the art of physiognomy, or reading character from physical features. The ancient Greeks compared the human face to various animals and birds, such as the eagle and the horse. They believed people shared certain character **traits** with the animals they resembled. A person with an equine, or horselike, face was thought to be loyal, brave, and **stern**. A person with an aquiline or eaglelike nose was believed to be bold and courageous, as well as **arrogant** and self-centered.

Physiognomists study such features as the shape of the head, the length and thickness of the neck, the color and thickness of the hair, and the shape of the nose, mouth, eyes, and chin. They believe that round-faced people are self-confident. **Prominent** cheekbones show strength of character, while a pointed nose reveals curiosity. Heavy, arched eyebrows belong to a decisive individual, while thin, arched eyebrows signal a restless and active personality. Almond-shaped eyes reveal an artistic nature. Round, soft eyes belong to dreamers. Down-turned lips reveal a proud character, while a long, pointed chin **indicates** someone who likes to give orders.

A related though not as ancient art is phrenology, the study of the bumps on the head. Phrenologists have identified forty bumps of various shapes and sizes on the human head. They "read" these bumps to identify a person's talents and character. For example, a bump between the nose and forehead is said to be present in people who have natural elegance and a love of beauty. A bump behind the curve of the ear is the sign of a courageous and adventurous person.

Phrenologists are not so much interested in health as they are in character and personality. They believe, for example, that a **bulge** in the center of the forehead is typical of people who have a good memory and a desire for knowledge. A small bump at the top of the head indicates a person who has strong moral character, while a bump just below this one is a sign of generosity and a kind, good nature. Phrenologists say a bump just above the tip of the eyebrow is found in people who love order and discipline, and a rise at the very back of the head is evident in people who are very attached to their families.

Phrenology was developed in the early eighteenth century by Franz Joseph Gall, a doctor in Vienna. His interest began at school when he noticed that boys with prominent eyes seemed to have the best memories. This led him to believe that a connection existed between appearance and ability. Dr. Gall's research interested many people, but he was **ridiculed** by other doctors. When he died in 1828, he was a poor and **bitter** man. It was only many years later that Dr. Gall's theories found support among doctors and scientists, and today the art of phrenology is still popular.

VOCABULARY

What are the meanings of the underlined words? Circle the letter of each correct answer.

1. A person's face can <u>reveal</u> a great deal about personality.
   a. show
   b. cover up
   c. hold

2. The ancient Greeks believed that people shared certain character <u>traits</u> with animals.
   a. features
   b. movements
   c. habits

3. A person with a horselike face might be proud and <u>stern</u>.
   a. noble
   b. serious
   c. quiet

4. A person with an eaglelike nose was believed to be <u>arrogant</u> and self-centered.
   a. honest
   b. proud
   c. lonely

5. <u>Prominent</u> cheekbones show strength of character.
   a. healthy
   b. hollow
   c. noticeable

6. A long, pointed chin <u>indicates</u> someone who likes to give orders.

    a. covers up

    b. points out

    c. encourages

7. A <u>bulge</u> in the center of the forehead is typical of people with a good memory.

    a. lump

    b. hole

    c. point

8. Dr. Gall was <u>ridiculed</u> by other doctors.

    a. praised

    b. questioned

    c. laughed at

9. He died a poor and <u>bitter</u> man.

    a. wishful

    b. unhappy

    c. faithful

COMPREHENSION

A. Looking for the Main Ideas

Circle the letter of the correct answer.

1. Physiognomists believe that

    _____.

    a. the head is the most important part of the body

    b. physical features reveal personality

    c. people are like animals in many ways

2. Phrenologists _____.

    a. "read" the bumps on people's heads to treat their health problems

    b. study bumps on the head to determine character traits

    c. believe the eyes are the "mirror of the soul"

3. Dr. Gall's ideas _____.

    a. were at first not accepted by other doctors

    b. were immediately considered the work of a genius

    c. are no longer popular

B. Looking for Details

Circle T if the sentence is true. Circle F if the sentence is false.

1. Physiognomy is a modern practice.   T   F
2. The ancient Greeks compared the human face to animals.   T   F
3. Phrenologists have identified twenty-five bumps on the head.   T   F
4. A bump on the forehead is a sign of courage.   T   F
5. Physiognomists study the shape of the head, face, and body.   T   F
6. Physiognomists believe that round-faced people are self-confident.   T   F
7. Phrenology is a much more ancient art than physiognomy.   T   F
8. Dr. Gall's research did not interest many people.   T   F
9. Dr. Gall was rewarded for his research later in life.   T   F

C. Making Inferences and Drawing Conclusions

The answers to the questions are not directly stated in the passage. Write complete answers.

1. Why did the Greeks compare humans to animals?
2. Why did other doctors ridicule Dr. Gall's research?
3. Why did Dr. Gall die a poor and bitter man?
4. What might a physiognomist say about someone with a long nose, thin eyebrows, and almond-shaped eyes?

DISCUSSION

Discuss these questions with your classmates.

1. What characteristics of the face and body show good health? What characteristics show bad health?
2. According to your astrological sign, what character traits are you supposed to have? Do you fit the description?
3. Do you think that astrology is more precise than physiognomy or phrenology?
4. Look at the diagram of the forty bumps on the head and examine your own bumps. How true is what the bumps reveal?

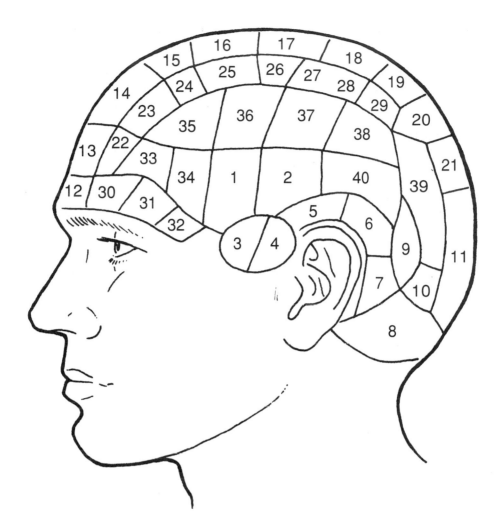

1. ***The music bump***
   This bump is a sign of a natural talent for music and artistic creativity.
2. ***The money bump***
   This bump shows the need to earn and save money.
3. ***The mathematics bump***
   This bump, which is in the center of the temple, is a sign of a scientific and logical mind.
4. ***The greed bump***
   This bump is found in people who are greedy about food and cannot control their appetites.
5. ***The business bump***
   This bump is a sign of a practical person with a good sense of business. People with a bump here find it hard to relax.
6. ***The courage bump***
   This bump is a sign of courage and adventure.

7. ***The strength bump***
   This bump appears in a person who has physical or mental energy.
8. ***The love bump***
   This bump appears in people who are passionate, jealous, or sensual.
9. ***The fighting bump***
   This bump reveals a competitive character in a person. This person is usually very determined to achieve something.
10. ***The affection bump***
    A bump here shows a person with an affectionate character who can love and show tenderness.
11. ***The parental bump***
    A protrusion in this area reveals that a person has a strong motherly or fatherly instinct.
12. ***The aesthetic bump***
    A bump here shows that a person has a strong love of beauty and elegance.

13. ***The studying bump***
    This bump is found in people who love knowledge and have a good memory.
14. ***The meditative bump***
    This appears in people who like to meditate and analyze.
15. ***The justice bump***
    This bump reveals a person who has a strong sense of what is right and what is wrong.
16. ***The kindness bump***
    A bump in this area is a sign of a person who is kind and generous.
17. ***The bump of spirituality***
    This bump on the top of the head shows that the person has a strong spiritual mind.
18. ***The bump of willpower***
    This bump shows willpower, determination, and reliability in a person.
19. ***The bump of authority***
    This bump is a sign of a person who likes to make decisions and control other people.
20. ***The bump of concentration***
    This bump belongs to a person with a strong ability to concentrate, particularly on intellectual matters.
21. ***The family bump***
    This bump appears in people who are attached to their families.
22. ***The travel bump***
    A bump in this area reveals someone who loves to travel and move from one place to another. This person will feel comfortable wherever he/she is.
23. ***The logic bump***
    This bump shows a logical person who has a strong sense of reasoning.
24. ***The flexible mind bump***
    A bump here shows that a person has an open and flexible mind.
25. ***The bump of conformity***
    This is the bump of someone who likes to conform to what is expected and obeys conventions, such as following the latest fashion.
26. ***The bump of idealism***
    This bump reveals a person who has strong ideals.
27. ***The bump of optimism***
    This bump shows that a person is optimistic about life and believes in other people.
28. ***The bump of success***
    A bump in this area indicates that a person puts all his/her efforts and energy into succeeding in life.
29. ***The critical bump***
    This bump shows that a person can look objectively at things and criticize himself/herself as well as others.
30. ***The objectivity bump***
    This bump is developed in people who can put themselves in someone else's place and be able to understand the other person's situation.
31. ***The color bump***
    This bump shows that a person has a strong sense of color as shown in either their clothes or surroundings.
32. ***The bump of meticulousness***
    This bump indicates a meticulous, orderly, neat, and precise person.
33. ***The organization bump***
    This bump is found in people who organize their time very efficiently so that not a moment is lost.
34. ***The rhythm bump***
    This bump is developed in musicians and singers who have a strong sense of rhythm.
35. ***The bump of gregariousness***
    This bump is seen in people who like to be with others and are very outwardly communicative, warm, and happy.
36. ***The originality bump***
    A bump in this area shows that a person has an original character and likes to be different and creative.
37. ***The inventive bump***
    This bump is a sign of a person who can create new things and be inventive.
38. ***The bump of fame***
    This bump shows that a person wants to be known and recognized by others. Many famous people have this bump.
39. ***The bump of caution***
    This bump belongs to a person who is very careful about everything.
40. ***The bump of tactfulness***
    This bump shows that a person is tactful, polite, and diplomatic with others.

WRITING

Read the following essay written by a student. Underline the thesis statement and the topic sentence in each of the body paragraphs.

A Virgo

Every person has both good and bad traits in their character. Most people do not like to be criticized by others. It is good to be honest with yourself. We must admit that we all have both good and bad traits and we must like ourselves as we are. If a person does not love even a part of themselves, then they are practically dead. Since I am going to write about myself, I will write about the good and bad traits of my character. I was born under the sign Virgo and I believe I have some of the characteristics of people born under this sign.

One example of a good trait of a Virgo that I have is patience. Sometimes I think I am almost too patient, but I have also found that patience helps me in a lot of things. For example, it helps me to study when the lesson is difficult or boring. Also, if I don't succeed in something, I am willing to try several more times. My patience also helps me to relax and stay calm. I am very patient with people too, e.g., I can work with children and senior citizens and even people who are sick and need a lot of help. I can deal with people who are nervous, angry, and upset and help them to calm down. Sometimes people take advantage of my patience, however, and I don't like that at all.

Another example of a trait that I have, which is typical of a Virgo, is ambition. I am very ambitious and can't sit in one place for more than ten minutes. If I make up my mind to do something, then I will do anything to meet my goal no matter how long it takes and how much energy and time will be needed to accomplish it. This is what helped me to graduate from high school in three years. I like to do housework, cook, and take care of babies. I also like to work outside my home. I like to be busy all day and have lots of things to do. This makes me happy and satisfied. I hate sitting at home all day doing nothing.

Finally, like anyone, Virgos have some bad traits too. This ambition can sometimes make them take on more work than they can handle, leading them to strain themselves to a breaking point. Sometimes I take on too much work and then reach a point at which I can do no more. Then I have to rest for a while and regain my strength. Virgos can also be fussy and irritable. I suppose I can be that way too sometimes. For instance, I like everything to be neat and tidy, and if someone comes along and messes things up, I will scold them.

In conclusion, I am very happy that I am a Virgo. My patience and ambition gave me the confidence I needed to choose to be a psychologist. Because I work hard and can deal with people who have problems, I think I will someday be very successful in this profession. Some people envy me for the traits I have and that gives me an idea, that I am not so bad after all.

ORGANIZING

The Example Essay

The student essay on page 51 is an example essay. Each paragraph gives an example to support the thesis statement.

To give examples, the following transitions can be used at the beginning of your paragraphs.

For the first body paragraph of your example essay:

> *One example of (noun phrase) is . . .*
> or *Take for example, . . .*
> or *An example of (noun phrase) is . . .*

For the second paragraph of your example essay:

> *Another example of (noun phrase) is . . .*
> or *An additional example is . . .*
> or *A second example of (noun phrase) is . . .*

For the last paragraph of your example essay:

> *A final example of (noun phrase) is . . .*
> *Finally, . . .*

If your last example is the most important:

> *The most important example of (noun phrase) is . . .*
> *The most significant/interesting example of (noun phrase) is . . .*

Now underline the transitions used to introduce examples in the body paragraphs of the student essay.

In your body paragraphs, you may use other specific examples to support your topic sentence. The following words and phrases introduce examples:

For example, _____sentence

_____.

or

For instance, _____sentence

_____.

For example and **for instance** have the same meaning. When your sentence begins with **for example** or **for instance**, put a comma after these words.

Remember, **for example** or **for instance** must be followed by a complete sentence.

> **For example,** it helps me to study when the lesson is difficult.

> **For instance,** I like everything to be neat and tidy.

Sometimes **e.g.** is used to show examples. **E.g.** is an abbreviation of the Latin *exempli grata*. **For example** and **e.g.** have the same meaning. Note the punctuation with **e.g.**

> I am very patient with people too, **e.g.**, I can work with children and senior citizens.
> or I am very patient with people too, **for example,** I can work with children and senior citizens.

When **for example, for instance,** or **e.g.** is used in the middle of a
sentence, use commas before and after these words.
For further examples, you may use **also** or **another**.

Exercise 1

*Complete the following with the correct transitions. There may be
more than one correct answer.*

The left and right sides of the face are quite different. Each side shows
different aspects of our personality. The left side of the face reveals the
instinctive and hereditary aspects of our personality. When we are under
stress, _____, with feelings like fear,
anger, or even intense happiness, force is put on the muscles of the left
side of the face. When we examine the left side of the face, our well-being
and troubles show up more. _____,
wrinkles on this side show the strong emotions we have experienced in our
lives. The right side of the face reflects our intelligence and self-control.
This side of the face is usually more relaxed and smoother. That is why,
_____, movie stars prefer to have this
side of their face photographed.

WRITING PRACTICE

Choose one of the following topics.

1. Give examples of your good and/or bad traits. Give specific
   examples of these traits.
2. Describe yourself according to the characteristics of your
   astrological sign.
3. Describe a person you know or would like to know using
   examples of two or three character traits.
4. Describe the character of a famous person using examples of
   his/her dominant character traits.

1. Pre-writing.

Work with a partner, a group, or alone.

1. Brainstorm the topic. Choose one of the pre-writing brainstorming
   techniques that you prefer.
2. Brainstorm for ideas about strong character traits.
3. Work on a thesis statement.

2. Outlining.

A. The next step is to organize your ideas.

Step 1: *Write your thesis statement.*

Step 2: *Pick the best examples of strong character traits.*

Step 3: *Remember to begin each paragraph with a transition showing example.*

B. Make a more detailed outline. The essay outline on page 17 will help you.

3. Write a rough draft.

4. Revise your rough draft.

Using the checklist below, check your rough draft or let your partner check it.

Essay Checklist

Essay Organization

Introduction: _____ General Statements
_____ Thesis Statement

Body: _____ Two or three paragraphs, each about a character trait.
_____ Begin paragraphs with transitions showing examples.

Conclusion: _____ Summary of main points or a statement of your thesis in other words and a final comment on topic.

Paragraph Organization

Topic Sentences: _____ Does each of your body paragraphs have a topic sentence with a controlling idea?

Supporting Sentences:
_____ Is each paragraph about one main idea? Do your sentences support your topic sentence?
_____ Do you have specific factual details and examples to support what you stated?

5. Edit Your Essay,

Work with a partner or a teacher to edit your essay. Correct spelling, punctuation, vocabulary, and grammar. Use the following editing symbols.

- cap   Capital letter
- sp   Spelling mistake
- sv   Mistake in agreement of subject and verb
- ^   Omission (You have left out something.)
- frag   Sentence fragment (Correct by completing sentence.)
- ro   Run-on sentence (Insert period and capital letter or add comma and conjunction.)

6. Write your final copy.

Chapter 6: The Many Faces of Medicine

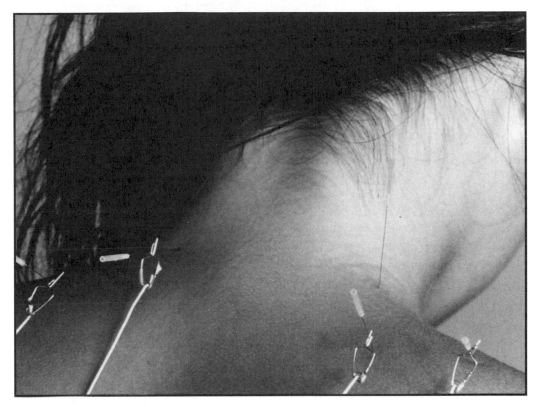

PRE-READING QUESTIONS

Discuss these questions with your classmates or teacher.

1 Why do you think the woman has needles in her neck?

2 How would you feel if this were done to you?

3 How many different approaches to medicine do you know about?

Reading: The Many Faces of Medicine

"**D**octor, I'm coughing and sneezing. I have itchy eyes, a drippy nose, and I ache all over. What's wrong with me? What should I do?"

"Take two aspirin and go to bed," one doctor advises.

"No, no. Drink this herbal tea," says another.

"Don't listen to them," argues the acupuncturist. "Come here and let me put some needles in your back."

Who has the best remedy? All of them, some people would say, because they believe that there is more than one **approach** to healing and many ways to practice medicine.

In general, modern medicine treats the body as if it were a machine made up of many separate parts that can break down **independently**. Treatment usually consists of trying to repair the broken part with drugs and surgery.

Holistic doctors take another approach. They believe that the parts of the body are interconnected and must be treated as a whole. For example, to treat a headache, these doctors might recommend massage to relax the body, get the blood flowing, and **relieve** the **tension** that is causing the headache.

Medical **practices** that do not depend on surgery and pharmaceutical drugs are called alternative forms of medicine. Some of these are more highly **respected** than others. For example, the Chinese method of acupuncture, although two thousand years old, is considered an effective remedy for **chronic** pain. On the other hand, the practice of reflexology, which uses foot massage to heal other parts of the body, might feel good, but there is little proof that it works.

Some forms of alternative medicine are centuries old. African herbalists have a long history of using tree bark, roots, grasses, and flowers to make teas to treat disease. Native Americans have used plant products to treat such illnesses as high blood pressure and coughs. At first, modern scientists laughed at herbal healers and called their methods "grandmother's remedies." Today, however, these same researchers are testing certain elements in plants for the possible treatment of cancer and AIDS.

Treatments that are unconventional, or out of the ordinary, have gained so much **prestige** and attention that the U.S. government has created an Office of Alternative Medicine. Researchers in this office study alternative forms of medicine in the United States and around the world. These include meditation, biofeedback, acupuncture, herbal medicine, hypnotism, homeopathy, and chiropractic medicine. In biofeedback, a machine is used to measure skin temperature and other responses. By watching the machine, a patient can learn to control muscle tension and blood pressure. Amazing results have come from the use of biofeedback, which has been successful in treating headaches, muscle pain, and even drug addiction. Homeopathy treats disease by giving a patient tiny amounts of a remedy that would produce symptoms similar to those of the disease in a healthy person. In Europe, this treatment has been known to help patients with flu, headaches, and allergies. People with back and muscle pain have been going to chiropractors for years, but it is only recently that chiropractors have received any kind of respect or recognition.

Many people have lost faith in modern medicine because researchers have been unable to find cures for a variety of problems, from cancer to the common cold. Some people turn to alternative medicine out of curiosity, others out of **desperation**. What many have realized is that often one treatment picks up where another leaves off. One medical technique can **complement** another. It seems likely that in the future the practice of medicine will consist of a combination of approaches drawn from a variety of cultures. Hopefully, this approach will prove to be the best one of all.

··

VOCABULARY

What are the meanings of the underlined words? Circle the letter of each correct answer.

1. There is more than one approach to healing and many ways to practice medicine.

   a. idea

   b. way of doing

   c. discussion

2. Modern medicine treats the body as if it were a machine made up of many parts that can break down independently.

   a. slowly

   b. separately

   c. together

3. A headache may be treated with massage to <u>relieve</u> the tension causing the headache.

    a. stop

    b. replace

    c. decrease

4. A massage relaxes the body and relieves the <u>tension</u> that is causing the headaches.

    a. tightness

    b. anger

    c. problem

5. Medical <u>practices</u> that do not depend on surgery and pharmaceutical drugs are called alternative forms of medicine.

    a. manners

    b. habits

    c. methods

6. Some forms of alternative medicine are more highly <u>respected</u> than others.

    a. admired

    b. controlled

    c. required

7. Acupuncture has been proved to be a very effective remedy for <u>chronic</u> pain.

    a. serious

    b. changing

    c. continual

8. Treatments that are unconventional have gained much <u>prestige</u> and attention.

    a. use

    b. importance

    c. profit

9. Some turn to alternative medicine out of curiosity, others out of <u>desperation</u>.

    a. hopelessness

    b. careful thought

    c. lack of ability

10. One medical technique can <u>complement</u> another.

    a. add to

    b. stay with

    c. take from

COMPREHENSION

A. Looking for the Main Ideas

Circle the letter of the best answer.

1. Medicine is a science that

    _____.

    a. can be practiced in more than one way

    b. should never be changed

    c. always uses surgery and drugs to heal people

2. Traditional medical doctors and holistic doctors

    _____.

    a. both treat the body as if it were a machine made up of independent parts

    b. have very different approaches to practicing medicine

    c. have lost faith in modern medicine

3. In the future, doctors will probably

    _____.

    a. stop using pharmaceutical drugs

    b. use machines to treat disease

    c. use several methods of treatment

B. Looking for Details

Scan the passage quickly to find the answers to these questions. Write complete answers.

1. What approach to holistic doctors take to healing the body?
2. Give two examples of the use of alternative medicine.
3. Name two forms of alternative medicine that are highly respected.
4. Name one form of medicine for which we do not have proof that it works.
5. List three things that African herbalists use to make medicine.
6. For approximately how long have the Chinese been practicing acupuncture?
7. Name five treatments being studied by researchers at the U.S. Government's Office of Alternative Medicine.
8. Explain how biofeedback works.

C. Making Inferences and Drawing Conclusions

The answers to these questions are not directly stated in the passage. Write complete answers.

1. Why might someone turn to alternative medicine?
2. Why have unconventional forms of medicine gained prestige?
3. If a patient had an ulcer, how might a holistic doctor treat it?
4. Why are some forms of alternative medicine more respected than others?

DISCUSSION

Discuss these questions with your classmates.

1. What form of medicine does your doctor practice?
2. Do you think a combination of different approaches to medicine is a good idea?
3. What do you think a doctor's office in the future will look like?

ORGANIZING

Such as

Another way to provide an example is by the use of **such as**. We use **such as** + example when we wish to be brief.

Examples

1. Practices **such as** acupuncture are common in holistic medicine.

2. Some forms of alternative medicine, **such as** herbal healing, are centuries old.

Note: 1. No commas are needed when the **such as** phrase gives essential information.

2. Use commas when the **such as** phrase can be taken out without changing the meaning of the sentence.

Exercise 1

Combine the two sentences into one sentence using* such as. *Use correct punctuation.

1. Some uses of biofeedback have been successful. For instance, the treatments for headaches, muscle pain, and drug addiction have been successful.

   Some uses of biofeedback, such as the treatments for headaches, muscle pain, and drug addiction, have been successful.

2. African herbalists use parts of a tree to make teas. For example, African herbalists use the bark to make teas.

3. Some forms of alternative medicine are highly respected. For example, the practice of acupuncture is highly respected.

4. There are many forms of alternative medicine from among which researchers today can choose. Herbal medicine, homeopathy, and chiropractic medicine are some examples.

5. Some practices feel good, but there is little proof that they work. An example of this type of practice is reflexology.

6. Homeopathy helps patients. For example, it helps patients with problems such as headaches and allergies.

Exercise 2

Punctuate these sentences containing examples.

1. Homeopathy for instance is a type of alternative medicine.
2. Biofeedback is successful in treating the following headaches, muscle pain and even drug addiction.
3. For instance they might use massage to treat a headache.
4. Chiropractic medicine is particularly helpful for treating problems such as back pain and muscle pain.
5. As an example chicken soup is a familiar grandmother's remedy for a cold in the United States.
6. In some European countries e g France homeopathy is popular.

Choose one of the following topics.

1. Choose two natural products (e.g., garlic, ginseng) and give examples of the problems they can be used to treat.

2. Give examples of how a health problem can be treated in two or more different ways.

3. Describe two or three "grandmother's" remedies. Tell what they are used for and whether they work.

1. Pre-writing.

Work with a partner, a group, or alone.

1. Brainstorm the topic. Choose a pre-writing technique that you prefer.

2. Work on a thesis statement.

2. Outlining.

A. The next step is to organize your ideas.

Step 1: *Write your thesis statement.*

Step 2: *Pick the two or three best examples from your brainstorming activity.*

Step 3: *Remember to use a variety of words and phrases to show examples.*

B. Make a more detailed outline.

3. Write a rough draft.

4. Revise your rough draft.

Using the checklist below, check your rough draft or let your partner check it.

Essay Checklist

Essay Organization

Introduction:	_____ General Statements
	_____ Thesis Statement
Body:	_____ Each body paragraph should show a clear example of a product or remedy.
	_____ Use transitions to show examples.
Conclusion:	_____ Summary of main points or a statement of your thesis in other words and a final comment on the topic.

Paragraph Organization

Topic Sentences:	_____ Does each of your body paragraphs have a topic sentence with a controlling idea?
Supporting Sentences:	
	_____ Is each paragraph about one main idea? Do your sentences support your topic sentence?
	_____ Do you have specific details or examples to support what you have stated?

5. Edit Your Essay.

Work with a partner or a teacher to edit your essay. Correct spelling, punctuation, vocabulary, and grammar. Use the following editing symbols.

- cap   Capital letter
- sp   Spelling mistake
- sv   Mistake in agreement of subject and verb
- ^   Omission (You have left something out.)
- frag   Sentence fragment (Correct by completing sentence.)
- ro   Run-on sentence (Insert period and capital letter or add comma and conjunction.)

6. Write your final copy.

Circle the letter of the best answer.

1. How long does it take for the blood to circulate throughout the body when you rest?

    a. two minutes

    b. sixty seconds

    c. forty seconds

2. The body burns calories fastest when you exercise within

    _____.

    a. three hours after a meal

    b. six hours after a meal

    c. eight hours after you sleep

3. When smoking a cigarette, the nicotine found in the tobacco reaches the brain in _____.

    a. one minute

    b. fifteen seconds

    c. seven seconds

4. We lose an eyelash every

    _____.

    a. three to five months

    b. six to eight months

    c. one to two weeks

5. Your gums are renewed every

    _____.

    a. six to eight months

    b. three to five years

    c. one to two weeks

6. Fingernails grow _____.

    a. as fast as toenails

    b. four times as fast as toenails

    c. twice as fast as toenails

UNIT 4

People

Chapter 7: The Shakers

PRE-READING QUESTIONS

Discuss these questions with your classmates or teacher.

 Describe the picture. What country do you think it is?

 Why do you think the people in the picture are dressed in this way?

3 Do you think men and women should live apart? Why or why not?

Reading: The Shakers

"Shake it up baby. Twist and shout," was sung by the Beatles, but it was practiced almost two hundred years earlier by a religious group called "The Unified Society of Believers." This religious group was founded in 1774 by Ann Lee who, with her followers, emigrated to America later that same year. The Believers worshiped by singing, dancing, shaking, and **whirling** around. Eventually they became known as "The Shakers."

The Shakers were a peaceful **sect** that welcomed people of all races. They were against war and lived in their own villages separate from the rest of society. They lived communally, that is, sharing their property and working for the common good. The qualities they admired were kindness, generosity, modesty, purity, cleanliness, and love for humanity. Their villages of plain white houses were so neat and tidy that even the roads were swept clean.

The Shakers are probably best known for their **celibacy** and **industriousness**. Single men and women did not marry. Married couples who joined the religion had to live apart. In the Shaker community, males and females lived in separate communal houses. They had strict rules regarding behavior between the sexes, such as never shaking hands or touching each other in any way. They ate, worked, and slept in separate **quarters**. When conversation between a man and a woman was necessary, it was done in the company of others. At their almost daily meetings for conversation and singing, males and females sat opposite each other. Even when they danced and whirled around during worship, men and women always kept their distance.

As might be expected, the Shaker style of dressing was modest, simple, and plain, and their clothes were dark in color. The women combed their hair back under a cap and wore long dresses with a cloth that covered the chest. Men wore dark pants and simple coats. Bright or attractive clothing was out of the question for these celibate people.

"Put your hands to work and your hearts to God," said Ann Lee to her followers. Those words were taken seriously by the Shakers, who were very hardworking people. In order to be **self-sufficient**, the Shakers grew their own food, wove their own cloth, and made their own tools, utensils, and handicrafts. They made chairs, buttons, tubs, baskets, smoking pipes, pens, brooms, brushes, hats, shoes, and hand-woven coats. Although simple and plain, these things were of the highest quality and the Shakers soon became famous for their superior products.

Not only were the Shakers industrious, but they were creative and inventive as well. Their long list of inventions and improvements includes such items as the flat broom, the common clothespin, the first garden seeds packaged in paper, and machines such as an improved washing machine, a revolving oven, and a wood-burning stove.

Although it may seem that Shaker life was all rules, work, and worship, their lives were not without joy. They spent pleasant hours gathering berries and picking fruit, walking in the woods, taking carriage rides, and laughing together—in separate groups, of course.

Over the years, the original Shaker community in New York expanded to twenty-four **scattered** among eight states in the eastern United States. Many people were attracted to their peaceful ways and clean crime-free villages. Eventually the Shakers paid a price for their celibacy, however, because without children to carry on their traditions and beliefs, their numbers eventually **dwindled** to a very few. Today, their villages are museums and their handicrafts are items for collectors. Nevertheless, the Shakers will not be forgotten. Their search for a perfect existence where everyone was equal and lived in **harmony** is recorded in American history. The Shakers will be remembered for their many fine products and inventions and for the **contribution** they made to society.

VOCABULARY

What are the meanings of the underlined words? Circle the letter of each correct answer.

1. The Shakers worshipped by dancing, shaking, and <u>whirling</u> around.

    a. rolling

    b. turning

    c. jumping

2. The Shakers were a peaceful <u>sect</u>.

    a. a group of people with special religious beliefs

    b. a group of people belonging to a secret organization

    c. a group of people who belong to a political party

3. The Shakers were known for their celibacy.

    a. marrying because of religious beliefs

    b. having large families

    c. not marrying because of religious beliefs

4. The Shakers were also known for their industriousness.

    a. hard work

    b. laziness

    c. businessmindedness

5. Shaker men and women ate, worked, and slept in separate quarters.

    a. houses

    b. gardens

    c. villages

6. The Shakers were almost totally self-sufficient.

    a. able to grow fruit and vegetables

    b. able to provide for their own needs without outside help

    c. able to keep alive on very little food

7. The Shaker communities expanded from the original one to twenty-four scattered among eight states.

    a. covered up

    b. grouped together

    c. spread out

8. Eventually, the Shakers dwindled in number.

    a. gradually became fewer

    b. gradually increased

    c. suddenly disappeared

9. In the Shaker community, everyone was equal and lived in harmony.

    a. melody

    b. agreement with each other

    c. groups

10. The Shakers will be remembered for the <u>contribution</u> they made to society.

    a. problem

    b. money

    c. gift

COMPREHENSION

A. Looking for the Main Ideas

Circle the letter of the correct answer.

1. The Shakers were _____.

    a. a religious group whose main belief was shaking

    b. a peaceful sect that lived communally

    c. not a true religious sect

2. The Shakers were known for their

    _____.

    a. farming methods

    b. decorated houses

    c. celibacy and hard work

3. Today, the Shakers _____.

    a. have dwindled in number to a few

    b. make handicrafts for museums

    c. have increased in number and live in villages that have become museums

B. Looking for Details

Scan the passage quickly to find the answers to these questions. Write complete answers.

1. Who founded the Shakers?
2. What qualities did the Shakers admire?
3. Under what conditions could a man have a conversation with a woman in the Shaker community?
4. What did a Shaker man wear?
5. What are some of the machines the Shakers invented?
6. What did the Shakers do for fun?

C. Making Inferences and Drawing Conclusions

The answers to these questions are not directly stated in the passage. Write complete sentences.

1. What would happen to a married couple with a child who joined the Shaker community?
2. Why do you think people joined the Shakers?
3. Why do you think they made such high-quality products?
4. Why did the Shakers want to be self-sufficient?
5. Why didn't the Shakers wear fashionable, colorful clothes?

DISCUSSION

Discuss these questions with your classmates.

1. What other religious or nonreligious communities have you heard about?
2. Why do you think people are happy living in these communities?
3. Would you like to live in a special community? If so, in one based on what idea?
4. Celibacy and industriousness were important characteristics of the Shakers. Do you think these are positive qualities? Why or why not?
5. Name a positive quality in a person. Explain why you think it is good.
6. Name a negative quality in a person. Explain why it is bad.

Now read the following essay written by a student. Underline the thesis statement and the topic sentence in each of the body paragraphs.

My Cousin Patricia

My cousin Patricia is a teacher and works for "Santa Maria de Fatima High School," in Peru. She has been teaching there for the last six years. She is thirty-two, but looks much younger. Patty is a very nice person to get along with, and has some very good qualities.

Patricia believes all people are equal. She likes to show people that women as well as men can do anything and be successful. When she talks about current events, she likes to mention the achievements of men and women of all races and nations. She often asks her students to do research on organizations in which people work together to make the world a better place.

My cousin is a good leader. If you ever had a chance to join any of her group meetings, you would notice right away how she enjoys leading others while encouraging them to participate in what is going on. When there are decisions to be made, she listens to everyone's opinions and respects their suggestions. People who know that aspect of her like her very much. People like to be with her and she has many friends. The only thing bad I can say about her is that I don't see her often enough.

In conclusion, my cousin Patty is very nice in many ways, is a very good teacher, and is the best company a person could have. I wish she didn't live so far away, but someday maybe she will come to live near my family. That will be a wonderful day.

The Dominant Impression

Often when describing people the **dominant impression** is used. The dominant impression is the main effect a person has on our feelings or senses. We get the dominant impression by selecting the most important feature or character trait of a person and emphasizing it. Adjectives like shy, beautiful, ambitious, or generous can easily give a dominant impression. This impression is then supported by details.

The first topic sentence in a paragraph will usually give you the dominant impression. Look at the student essay and underline the words in each of the topic sentences of the body paragraphs that give you the dominant impression.

Exercise 1

Look at the dominant impressions and the groups of sentences below. In each case, find the sentences that do not support the dominant impression.

1. Dominant impression: My brother is ambitious.
   a. He likes to watch the latest news on television.
   b. He takes extra classes at school.
   c. He's captain of his football team.
   d. He's already decided that he wants to be a doctor.
   e. He takes a trip to Switzerland every year.

2. Dominant impression: My best friend is shy.
   a. She never speaks to people when there's a party.
   b. She likes to read books a lot.
   c. She never raises her voice.
   d. She likes to wear green sweaters.
   e. She always disappears when I want to introduce her to someone.

3. Dominant impression: My aunt is thoughtful.
   a. She always remembers my birthday.
   b. She likes to work in the garden.
   c. She likes to listen to classical music and read poetry.
   d. She always offers me a cup of tea when I visit.
   e. She offers me a sweater when I'm cold.

Choose one of the following topics.

1. Describe yourself or someone you know using one or two adjectives to give the dominant impression.

2. Describe a group of people, a race, or a nation using one or two adjectives stereotyping the dominant impression.

1. Pre-writing.

Work with a partner, a group, or alone.

1. Brainstorm the topic. Choose a pre-writing technique you prefer.

2. Brainstorm for descriptive adjectives and supporting details for them.

3. Work on a thesis statement.

2. Outlining.

A. The next step is to organize your ideas.

Step 1: *Write your thesis statement.*

Step 2: *Pick one or two of the best descriptive adjectives from your brainstorming activity.*

Step 3: *Remember to find relevant details to support your dominant impression.*

B. Make a more detailed outline. The essay outline on page 17 will help you.

3. Write a rough draft.

4. Revise your rough draft.

Using the checklist below, check your rough draft or let your partner check it.

Essay Checklist

Essay Organization

Introduction: _____ General Statements
_____ Thesis Statement

Body: _____ Logical sequence of descriptive details.
_____ Establish a point of view, either first person (I, we) or third person (he, she, they), and keep to the same point of view throughout.

Conclusion: _____ Summary of main points or a statement of your thesis in other words and a final comment on the topic.

Paragraph Organization

Topic Sentence: _____ Does each of your body paragraphs have a topic sentence with a controlling idea?

Supporting Sentences:
_____ Is each paragraph about one main idea? Do your sentences support your topic sentence?
_____ Do you have specific details to support what you have stated?

5. Edit Your Essay,

Work with a partner or a teacher to edit your essay. Correct spelling, punctuation, vocabulary, and grammar. Use the following editing symbols.

- cap   Capital letter
- sp   Spelling mistake
- sv   Mistake in agreement of subject and verb
- ^   Omission (You have left something out.)
- frag Sentence fragment (Correct by completing sentence.)
- ro   Run-on sentence (Insert period and capital letter or add comma and conjunction.)

6. Write your final copy.

Chapter 8: A Long Journey for Gordon Parks

PRE-READING QUESTIONS

Discuss these questions with your classmates or teacher.

1. Describe the woman in the photograph.
2. This is a famous photograph. What do you think has made it so famous?
3. What does it tell you about the photographer?

Reading: A Long Journey for Gordon Parks

Gordon Parks, famous photographer, **honored** author, composer, and painter, rose from **humble** beginnings to international fame. Born in Kansas in 1912, he was the youngest of fifteen children. Parks' father was a humble, hardworking farmer. His mother was a **devoted** and religious woman who taught her children to believe in themselves and their ability to succeed even though they faced poverty and **prejudice**. She taught Parks the value of honor, education, equality, and honesty, and although she died when Parks was only sixteen, she was a great influence on his life.

After his mother's death, Parks went to St. Paul, Minnesota, to live with his sister and her husband. Life there was not good. Parks was unwelcome in his brother-in-law's home, and he soon found himself put out on the streets to survive on his own. He went to school during the day and **bussed** tables in the evening, the only kind of job an African-American could find in those days. Eventually he got a job as a **bellhop**, but he was soon out of work again, like thousands of people, during a very bad economic time known as the Great Depression. Parks went to live with another sister and her two children, and together they somehow managed to survive the hard times. Although he was out of work, he kept himself busy practicing on the piano, writing songs, painting, and reading every book he could find.

Parks eventually got a job bussing tables at a big hotel where the orchestra played his songs and offered him a job playing the piano. But soon the orchestra moved on and Parks was back to bussing tables again. Finally, by then a husband and father, Parks got a job as a waiter on passenger trains. During a stopover in Chicago one day, he went to a movie house where Norman Alley, a photographer who shot **newsreel** pictures, went onstage to talk about his experiences. Parks was so impressed that he decided at that moment to become a photographer.

A few days later, Parks bought a second-hand camera and taught himself how to use it. Several store owners were so impressed by his photographs that they agreed to display them in their store windows. This eventually led to many job offers. Later, Parks went to Chicago where he did fashion photography. While this earned him a living, his real interest was in taking pictures of ordinary people, especially African-American families. The hardships Parks **endured** in his lifetime and his battle against racism helped him to understand people and to **capture** their emotions and personalities in his pictures.

Parks took pictures everywhere he went. When he had a large collection, he applied for a **grant** from the Julius Rosenwald Fund and was awarded enough money to study photography for a year. He went to Washington, D.C., where he was accepted into the Farm Security Administration (FSA), which had been set up by President Franklin Roosevelt to help **struggling** farmers. FSA photographers were hired to create a picture history of life in America during the Depression. Parks was the only African-American photographer working there, and over the years he opened the way for future African-American photographers.

Parks learned a lot while working for the FSA, and when it was shut down, he went to work for the Office of War Information. Parks wrote two books on photography, and in 1949 he was hired by *Life* magazine. As a *Life* magazine photographer, Parks traveled all over the world, taking pictures of important people and places and winning many awards for his work. He wrote four more books, one of which was *The Learning Tree*, a story based on his own life growing up in a small Kansas town. It was made into a movie that Parks himself directed.

Parks didn't stop there. He continued to take photographs, write articles and books, make movies, and compose music. In 1988, at the age of seventy-five, President Ronald Reagan presented Parks with the National Medal of Arts. When Parks was asked for a comment, he simply said, "It's been a long journey."

VOCABULARY

What are the meanings of the underlined words? Circle the letter of each correct answer.

1. Gordon Parks rose from humble beginnings to international fame.
   a. gentle
   b. simple
   c. uneducated

2. Gordon Parks was an honored author, composer, and painter.
   a. respected
   b. proud
   c. personal

3. His mother was a devoted and religious woman.
   a. educated
   b. clean
   c. dutiful

4. The Parks family faced poverty and prejudice.

    a. unfairness

    b. crime

    c. hunger

5. Gordon Parks bussed tables in the evening.

    a. made

    b. transported

    c. cleaned

6. He got a job as a bellhop in a hotel.

    a. a person who helps guests to their rooms and carries their luggage

    b. a person who cleans hotel rooms

    c. a person who works in the hotel kitchen

7. Normal Alley was a photographer who shot newsreel pictures.

    a. color photographs

    b. movie films of news

    c. real pictures

8. Parks endured many hardships in his lifetime.

    a. avoided

    b. understood

    c. put up with

9. Parks' experience helped him capture people's emotions in his pictures.

    a. catch

    b. win

    c. remember

10. Parks applied for a grant from the Julius Rosenwald Fund.

    a. permission to work

    b. money for support

    c. contest

11. The FSA was set up to help struggling farmers.

    a. trying to survive

    b. uneducated

    c. religious

A. Looking for the Main Ideas

Circle the letter of the best answer.

1. The person who influenced Parks' life most was

   _____.

   a. his mother

   b. his father

   c. his sister

2. When he went to Washington, D.C., Parks

   _____.

   a. did fashion photography

   b. was a photographer for the FSA

   c. played the piano

3. Toward the end of his life, Parks was

   _____.

   a. given a grant by the FSA

   b. hired by *Life* magazine

   c. presented with the National Medal of Arts

B. Looking for Details

Circle T if the sentence is true. Circle F if the sentence is false.

1. Gordon Parks was a photographer, painter, author, and composer.	T	F
2. Parks was one of sixteen children.	T	F
3. The FSA was set up to help farmers.	T	F
4. Parks traveled all over the world for the FSA.	T	F
5. Parks wrote two books on photography in 1949.	T	F
6. Parks directed a movie about himself.	T	F
7. Ronald Reagan said to Parks, "It's been a long journey."	T	F

C. Making Inferences and Drawing Conclusions

The answers to these questions are not directly stated in the passage. Write complete sentences.

1. Why do you think bussing tables was the only kind of job an African-American could find in those days?

2. Why did Parks apply for a grant?

3. What do you think Parks learned while working for the FSA?

4. Why was Parks interested in taking pictures of ordinary people?

5. Why did Parks comment, ''It's been a long journey''?

DISCUSSION

Discuss these questions with your classmates.

1. What other famous people do you know who have risen from difficult beginnings?

2. Who are the people who have a great influence on our lives?

3. Who has influenced your life and in what way?

WRITING

ORGANIZING

The story of Gordon Parks is a **narrative**. A narrative relates the story of events or action. Narrative puts events in time and tells us what happened according to a natural time sequence.

In a narrative, time order words and phrases are used to show the order in which events happen.

- first, second, etc.
- then
- next
- finally
- afterward
- meanwhile
- soon
- eventually
- when
- a few days later
- one day
- after a while
- in 1988

Note: Time order words and phrases at the beginning of a sentence are followed by a comma.

Now read ''A Long Journey for Gordon Parks'' and underline all the time order words and phrases.

The following sentences about Gordon Parks are not in the correct time order. Number the sentences in the correct order.

_____ Parks went to St. Paul, Minnesota, to live with his sister.

_____ Gordon Parks was born on November 30, 1912.

_____ Parks worked for the FSA in Washington, D.C.

_____ Parks was hired by *Life* magazine.

_____ Parks went to school during the day and bussed tables in the evening.

_____ He went to a movie house and was impressed by the photographer Norman Alley.

_____ Parks bought a second-hand camera.

_____ Parks got a job as a waiter on passenger trains.

_____ His pictures were displayed in store windows.

_____ He received a grant from the Julius Rosenwald Fund.

_____ Parks was presented with the National Medal of Arts.

_____ He earned a living as a fashion photographer in Chicago.

Using Description with Narrative

Often, we do not use one form of writing alone. For example, a story, which is usually a narrative, will have descriptions of people and places. From the Gordon Parks story, here are some examples of description.

Examples:

Parks' father was a humble, hardworking farmer.
His mother was a devoted and religious woman.
Life there was not good.

We use **adjectives** to describe people and places. Adjectives modify nouns.

Parks' father was a <u>humble</u>, <u>hardworking</u> <u>farmer</u>.
                       adj   adj   noun

His mother was a <u>devoted</u> and <u>religious</u> <u>woman</u>.
                    adj   adj   noun

<u>Life</u> there was not <u>good</u>.
noun   adj

Exercise 2

Underline all the adjectives in "A Long Journey for Gordon Parks."
Then twice underline the nouns they modify.

WRITING PRACTICE

Choose one of the following topics.

1. Write the story of your life or of the life of a person you know.
2. Write the story of a famous person.
3. Describe how someone influenced your life.

1. Pre-writing.

Work with a partner, a group, or alone.

1. Brainstorm the topic. Choose a pre-writing technique that you prefer.
   Write down important events in your or someone else's life.
2. Work on a thesis statement.

2. Outlining.

A. The next step is to organize your ideas.

Step 1: *Write a thesis statement.*

Step 2: *Arrange the events in the correct order.*

Step 3: *Decide whether you will tell the story in the first person (I, we) or in the third person (he, she, they). Remember to keep the same person throughout your story.*

B. Make a more detailed outline. Remember to use some description in your story.

3. Write a rough draft.

4. Revise your rough draft.

Using the checklist below, check your rough draft or let your partner check it.

Essay Checklist

Essay Organization

Introduction:	_____ General Statements
	_____ Thesis Statement
Body:	_____ Logical order of events
	_____ Use of time words to show order of events
Conclusion:	_____ The end of the story or the result of the events

Paragraph Organization

Topic Sentences:	_____ Does each of the body paragraphs show a sequence of events?
Supporting Sentences:	
	_____ Do your sentences describe or give details to illustrate the events?
	_____ Do you have specific details to support what you have said?

5. Edit Your Essay,

Work with a partner or a teacher to edit your essay. Correct spelling, punctuation, vocabulary, and grammar. Use the following editing symbols.

- cap Capital letter
- sp Spelling mistake
- sv Mistake in agreement of subject and verb
- ^ Omission (You have left something out.)
- frag Sentence fragment (Correct by completing sentence.)
- ro Run-on sentence (Insert period and capital letter or add comma and conjunction.)

6. Write your final copy.

Circle T if the sentence is true. Circle F if the sentence is false.

1. The first woman in space was an American, Sally Ride.   T   F

2. The largest manufacturer of sports clothes in the world,   T   F
   Adidas, was started by a German, Adolf Dasler, in the
   1920s.

3. The gypsies, who number five million people today,   T   F
   originally came from Egypt.

4. Only three people have received Oscar nominations for both   T   F
   best screenwriter and best actor. The first was Charlie
   Chaplin, the second was Orson Welles, and the third was
   Sylvester Stallone.

5. David Attenborough invented the aqualung, produced the   T   F
   world's first underwater camera, and then started making
   underwater films for TV.

6. Seiji Ozawa is a world-famous conductor from Japan.   T   F

UNIT 5

Food

Chapter 9: A Variety of
American Foods

PRE-READING QUESTIONS

Discuss these questions with your classmates or teacher.

1. Look at the two pictures and tell how they are different.

2. How might the lifestyles in these areas be different?

3. What kinds of foods do you think the people in each of these areas eat?

Reading: A Variety of American Foods

The French are famous for their sauces, the Italians praised for their pasta, the Germans **celebrated** for their sausages, but is there anything unique to eat in the United States? When you get right down to it, there's nothing quite as un-American as American food. Because the United States is made up mostly of immigrants, there is an amazing variety of foods, from clam chowder in Boston to chile con carne in Houston. The United States is a vast country influenced by many cultures and climates, and the traditional food of one area is often totally unlike that of another. New Mexico and Massachusetts are good examples of states that have very different traditional foods.

To understand and appreciate the food in any one region, it often helps to know the area's history. For example, New Mexico was once the home of the Pueblo Indians who lived in villages and grew native crops such as corn, beans, pumpkins, and squash. Later, Spanish settlers arrived in this area. These two groups exchanged ideas and customs and passed these customs on to their descendants. This intermingling of cultures is evident in the food of New Mexico.

New Mexican meals make much use of corn, which is served in a variety of ways—baked as tortillas, served fresh as **corn on the cob, blended** into soups and sauces, and mixed into salads or with other vegetables, especially red and green peppers. Native blue corn is quite surprising when it is served as blue corn bread, chips, or tortillas. In the markets of New Mexico, you can still find *chicos*, or sun-dried grains of roast sweet corn. *Chicos* last a long time, but when **soaked** and boiled, they taste almost like fresh corn. Many recipes also contain *pinon* or pine nuts, the small sweet seeds of the southwestern pine tree, once a **staple** food in the Pueblo diet.

A Spanish influence can be found in the sweet, anise-flavored cookies sold in New Mexican bakeries. They are prepared much like they were made in the kitchens of seventeenth-century Spain for the Christmas feast.

Some traditional foods of New Mexico that show both a native American and Spanish **heritage** include enchiladas (corn tortillas **stuffed** with cheese, onions, tomatoes, and chilies, and sometimes chicken or beef), pinto beans, black beans, and hot and spicy salsa, an uncooked vegetable sauce.

Take a trip to Massachusetts, however, and not a chili pepper nor a tortilla will you find in a traditional meal. Influenced by the cold climate and the English-speaking people who settled there, the **New England** kitchen gives off the aromas of soups and stews and of meat that is roasted for hours in the oven. Potatoes, carrots, and turnips were popular because these root vegetables grew well in the region and could be stored all winter long in the days before supermarkets and refrigerators. English-style puddings and pies are traditional desserts rather than the fresh fruit one often gets in the Southwest.

Whereas beef and chicken appear in many New Mexican recipes, in Massachusetts fish is very popular because of the nearby seacoast. New England is famous for its clam chowder, lobster, cod, scallops, and fish cakes. English herbs and spices are the seasonings used in New England dishes, which might taste rather **bland** to people accustomed to hot and spicy New Mexican food.

Each region of the United States is unique. Louisiana has a French influence. Many Germans populate the Midwest. In traveling around America, a tourist has the opportunity not only to visit a variety of places and see **diverse** landscapes, but to taste a variety of foods as well. Some may be very different. Others will taste just like home.

VOCABULARY

What are the meanings of the underlined words? Circle the letter of each correct answer.

1. The Germans are celebrated for their sausages.
    a. appreciated
    b. concerned
    c. well known

2. Corn on the cob is served in New Mexico.
    a. chopped corn
    b. whole ear of corn
    c. crushed corn

3. In New Mexico, corn is blended into soups.
    a. mixed
    b. poured
    c. drained

4. When chicos are soaked and boiled, they taste like fresh corn.
    a. left in water
    b. cut into small pieces
    c. dried in the sun

5. Pine nuts were a <u>staple</u> food in the Pueblo Indians' diet.

    a. hard to find

    b. cultivated

    c. eaten often

6. Some foods of New Mexico show both a Native and a Spanish American <u>heritage</u>.

    a. flavor

    b. tradition

    c. condition

7. Enchiladas are corn tortillas <u>stuffed</u> with cheese, onions, tomatoes, and chilies.

    a. melted

    b. eaten

    c. filled

8. The <u>New England</u> kitchen gives off the aromas of soups and stews.

    a. the southwestern United States

    b. the northeastern United States

    c. the Midwest area of America

9. New England food might taste <u>bland</u> to some people.

    a. tasteless

    b. spicy

    c. flavorful

10. America has a <u>diverse</u> landscape.

    a. much of the same

    b. many differences

    c. changes in size

A. Looking for the Main Ideas

Circle the letter of the best answer.

1. America _____.

    a. has lots of typical foods

    b. has not shared many customs with other people

    c. has been influenced by many cultures

2. Food in America _____.

    a. is the same from coast to coast

    b. is mostly hot and spicy

    c. changes from one place to another

3. To appreciate the food in a region,

    _____.

    a. it helps to know the area's history

    b. it's important to see the landscape

    c. a tourist has to travel to many areas

B. Looking for Details

Circle T if the sentence is true. Circle F if the sentence is false.

1. The Spanish settlers and Pueblo Indians in New Mexico shared their customs.   T   F

2. The Spanish brought corn to the Pueblo Indians.   T   F

3. Corn is only served on special occasions in New Mexico.   T   F

4. Lobster is a favorite dish in New Mexico.   T   F

5. In America, the traditional food of one area is often very different from that of another area.   T   F

6. Beef was a stable food of the Native Americans.   T   F

7. Climate has an influence on the type of food eaten in certain areas.   T   F

8. Food in Louisiana has been influenced by the French.   T   F

9. New England is famous for its clam chowder.   T   F

10. Fresh fruit is only popular in the Northeast.   T   F

C. Making Inferences and Drawing Conclusions

The answers to these questions are not directly stated in the passage. Write complete sentences.

1. Why are the foods in different regions of the United States so different?

2. How does the history of an area help us to appreciate the food that is eaten there?

3. Why is the food in New Mexico often hot and spicy?

4. Why do so many New England meals consists of hearty foods like stews and roasts and puddings and pies?

5. What kinds of food might a person find in the Midwest?

DISCUSSION

Discuss these questions with your classmates.

1. Describe the similarities and differences between two or more regions in your country. (Are there differences in climate? In geography?)

2. Describe two types of cuisines in your country.

3. What do you think about food in America?

4. Compare breakfast in your country with breakfast in the United States.

Read the following essay written by a student. Underline the thesis statement and the topic sentences in each of the body paragraphs.

Food Customs in Iran

Food customs around the world are strongly connected to culture, tradition, and geography. We can see this in my country, Iran. It has a variable climate, which gives us the advantage of having a large variety of foods to eat. However, what we eat is still influenced by our traditions and geography, as we can see in the similarities and differences between the north and south of Iran.

Many of the food customs are similar everywhere in the country. For example, in both northern and southern Iran, food is eaten with one's hand and a piece of bread instead of using utensils. Rice is an important staple in Iran and it is a part of almost every meal in both the north and south. Another similarity between the north and south is eating fish since both areas are near seas: the Caspian Sea in the north and the Persian Gulf in the south.

Because the north of Iran is quite different from the south, there are several differences in eating habits between the two areas. Northern Iran faces the Caspian Sea where we find the special fish from which the famous caviar is made, and which northerners love to eat. Because of the Mediterranean climate in the north, rice is one of the major crops and it plays an important role at the table in northern Iran. It is served at all ceremonies. As a tradition, northerners conduct a rice ceremony every year by putting rice-twigs in the paddy and singing songs. In southern Iran, which faces the Persian Gulf, a variety of seafoods, especially the white fish, make up the favorite dishes. Although rice is important and a part of most meals, the south is better known for its vegetables and fruits. Dates, in particular, are important, and are a major export to Western countries.

In conclusion, Iran is a large country with a diverse geography and people. As in all large countries, a variety of customs can be found on all points of the compass. Food customs in particular are influenced by climate and location, making Iran a very interesting country in which to live and eat!

ORGANIZING

Comparing and Contrasting

In this unit, you will learn how to organize a comparison and contrast essay.

1. When we **compare**, we look at the similarities between two things, people, or ideas. When we **contrast**, we look at the differences. It is important to remember these points when comparing and contrasting:

2. The two things that you compare and contrast must be of the same general class. You could not compare and contrast a mouse with an elephant, but you could compare and contrast the African elephant with the Indian elephant.

3. When you compare and contrast two things, the points you use for support must be used for both things. For example, if you write about the vegetables and fruit, the ways of cooking, and the use of spices in one area, you must also discuss these points about another area.

There are several ways of organizing your comparison and contrast essay. In this chapter, we will look at the most basic pattern, which is called **block organization**.

In block organization, all the similarities are discussed in one block (one or more paragraphs). Then the differences are discussed in another block. The block organization pattern looks like this:

Topic: The Similarities and Differences of the Food of the North and the South of China

I. Similarities

> A. Basic ingredients
> B. Use of spices
> C. Famous dishes

II. Differences

> A. Basic ingredients
> B. Use of spices
> C. Famous dishes

Comparison and Contrast Words

In order to write a good comparison and contrast essay, it is important to use the correct comparison and contrast words to introduce your points. The following is a list of some of the words and phrases.

Contrast words and phrases

Sentence Connectors	Clause Connectors	Others
similarly likewise also too	as just as and	like (+ noun) similar to (+ noun) just like (+ noun) (be) similar to (be) same as both . . . and not only . . . but also

Contrast words and phrases

Sentence Connectors	Clause Connectors	Others
however nevertheless in contrast on the other hand on the contrary	although even though while whereas	but yet despite (+ noun) in spite of (+ noun)

Using *While* and *Whereas*

While and **whereas** have the same meaning and are both used in the same way. Both words are used to show that something is in contrast to or directly the opposite of something else. They can be used at the beginning or at the end of a sentence.

> The meat is sweet, **whereas** the vegetables are salty.
> The meat is sweet, **while** the vegetables are salty.
> **While** the vegetables are salty, the meat is sweet.
> **Whereas** the vegetables are salty, the meat is sweet.

While and **whereas** can be used with either idea with no change in meaning. Note the use of commas with **while** and **whereas**.

Exercise 1

Join the two sentences using while *or* whereas *at the beginning of the sentence. Use the correct punctuation.*

1. In New Mexico, fresh fruit is popular for dessert. In New England, pies are often served.

2. In New Mexico, peppers and corn are popular as vegetables. In New England, potatoes and carrots are eaten.

3. In New Mexico, chicken and beef appear in many recipes. In New England, fish is popular in many dishes.

4. The British put milk in their tea. The Chinese drink it plain.

5. The Chinese love to stir-fry and deep fry. The Vietnamese prefer to steam food or eat it raw.

6. The Chinese and Vietnamese use chopsticks that are about nine inches long and round at the eating end. The Japanese prefer shorter chopsticks that have a pointed end.

WRITING PRACTICE

Choose one of the following topics.

1. Compare and contrast the food in two areas or regions of your country.

2. Compare and contrast the way people eat in this country with the way people eat in your country.

3. Compare and contrast the way one kind of food (e.g., rice, bread) is eaten in different ways by different people.

1. Pre-writing.

Work with a partner, a group, or alone.

1. Brainstorm the topic. Choose a pre-writing technique you prefer.
2. Brainstorm for similarities and differences.
3. Work on a thesis statement.

2. Outlining.

A. The next step is to organize your ideas.

Step 1: *Write your thesis statement.*

Step 2: *Choose three good points of comparison and contrast from your brainstorming activity.*

Step 3: *Remember to put your three points of comparison and contrast in the same order in the body paragraphs.*

B. Make a more detailed outline. The essay outline on page 17 will help you.

3. Write a rough draft.

4. Revise your rough draft.

Using the checklist below, check your rough draft or let your partner check it.

Essay Checklist

Essay Organization

Introduction:	_____ General Statements
	_____ Thesis Statement
Body:	_____ Similarities and then differences. Use the same order of points for each.
	_____ Use of different transitions to show comparison and contrast.
Conclusion:	_____ Summary of main points or a statement of your thesis in other words and a final comment on the topic.

Paragraph Organization

Topic Sentence: _____ Does each of your body paragraphs have a topic sentence with a controlling idea?

Supporting Sentences:

_____ Is each paragraph about one main idea? Do your sentences support your topic sentence?

_____ Do you have specific details or examples to support what you have stated?

5. Edit Your Essay,

Work with a partner or a teacher to edit your essay. Correct spelling, punctuation, vocabulary, and grammar. Use the following editing symbols.

- cap Capital letter
- sp Spelling mistake
- sv Mistake in agreement of subject and verb
- ^ Omission (You have left something out.)
- frag Sentence fragment (Correct by completing sentence.)
- ro Run-on sentence (Insert period and capital letter or add comma and conjunction.)

6. Write your final copy.

Chapter 10: Tea, Anyone?

PRE-READING QUESTIONS

Discuss these questions with your classmates or teacher.

1 Can you identify which countries use each type of teaware?

2 How many different kinds of tea can you name?

3 What is the customary way of drinking tea in your country?

Reading: Tea, Anyone?

There is a saying that the British like a nice cup of tea in the morning and a nice cup of tea at night. And at half past seven, their idea of heaven is a nice cup of tea. They like a nice cup of tea with their dinner and a nice cup of tea with their tea, and before they go to bed, there's a lot to be said for a nice cup of tea!

Sometimes it seems that no one likes tea quite as much as the British do. But, in fact, tea is popular in countries around the world, and many different **rituals** and customs for drinking tea have developed over the centuries. In China and Japan, tea was first used as a medicine; it wasn't until many years later that people there drank tea as a **beverage**. Because tea had been considered a sacred remedy, it was always served with much ceremony.

When the Chinese first started drinking tea, they didn't use teapots. Instead, they put tea leaves and hot water into a small bowl with a cover. Drinkers would bring the bowl to their lips and lift the cover very slightly with their forefingers, just enough to drink the liquid but not the leaves. People drank tea in this way **regardless** of the occasion, and it was always offered to guests.

Tea drinking was an important part of Chinese life, but nowhere in the world did people drink tea with more ceremony than in Japan. There, a strict ritual was set down in the fifteenth century by the first great tea master, Shuko. This tea ceremony is still performed today. Guests must wash their hands and faces and remove their shoes before entering the tearoom through a low doorway that forces them to **stoop** and appear **humble**. As the guests sit cross-legged on mats, the host places a spoonful of powdered tea into a special bowl, adds boiling water, and then stirs it with a bamboo **whisk**. Although in early tea ceremonies, everyone drank from the same bowl, it later became the practice for the host to serve the tea in individual bowls. The guests sip the tea slowly and talk until they have finished drinking. Then they are expected to throw back their heads and take the final sip with a loud sound to show how good the tea is. As the ceremony comes to an end, the guests admire the empty serving bowl for its beauty. The host washes the cups and the ceremony ends. The formal tea ceremony is certainly not **undertaken** every time someone drinks tea in Japan, but the tea is always served with much care and politeness.

The British also like to be formal and **dignified** when they serve tea. While the Japanese serve green tea in small cups without handles, the British favor the black teas of India and Ceylon served in china cups with handles and matching saucers. In Britain, tea is made in a pot, using one teaspoonful of tea leaves for each cup plus one extra teaspoonful for the pot. Boiling water is poured into the pot and the tea is left for about five minutes before the host pours for the guests. As in Japan, tea drinking is an important part of daily life in England. Many people drink tea several times a day and they associate it with relaxation and entertainment. Sharing a cup of tea with guests provides an opportunity for conversation and a quiet moment away from the normal **hustle and bustle**.

Many interesting tea customs have developed over the centuries. In Korea, for example, you might see someone eating a raw egg between sips of tea. The Burmese soak tea leaves in oil and garlic and eat this mixture with dried fish. In Thailand, people chew tea leaves seasoned with salt and other spices. In Iran, perfumed tea is a favorite. It is made by leaving flowers or herbs in the tea container for several days. In Morocco, tea is prepared in a brass or silver teapot to which sugar and mint are added. Then the tea is served in small glasses with mint leaves. If guests accept an offer of tea, they are expected to drink at least three glasses.

Regardless of where or how tea is prepared and served, many people consider it to be an important part of their social life. Having a cup of tea provides a reason for getting together and sharing a moment of conversation. Tea may no longer be considered a sacred cure for all illnesses, but it is a remedy for both the body and spirit in our sometimes **frantic** lives.

VOCABULARY

What are the meanings of the underlined words? Circle the letter of each correct answer.

1. Many <u>rituals</u> and customs have developed over the centuries.

    a. habits

    b. stories

    c. ceremonies

2. It was many years before tea was taken as a <u>beverage</u>.

    a. drink

    b. medicine

    c. food

3. Tea was taken in this way <u>regardless</u> of the occasion.

    a. in spite of

    b. because of

    c. depending upon

4. Guests enter through a low doorway that forces them to <u>stoop</u>.

    a. fall

    b. bend over

    c. lift their head

5. The low doorway forces them to stoop and appear <u>humble</u>.

    a. obedient

    b. proud

    c. strong

6. The host stirs the tea with a bamboo <u>whisk</u>.

    a. spoon

    b. beater

    c. knife

7. The tea ceremony is not <u>undertaken</u> every time tea is served in Japan.

    a. expected

    b. completed

    c. performed

8. The British also like to be formal and <u>dignified</u>.

    a. important

    b. well-mannered

    c. strict

9. Tea provides a quiet moment away from the <u>hustle and bustle</u>.

    a. problems

    b. rush

    c. children

10. Tea is a remedy for our body and spirit in our sometimes <u>frantic</u> lives.

    a. very unhealthy

    b. calm and quiet

    c. extremely busy

A. Looking for the Main Ideas

Circle the letter of the correct answer.

1. Tea is popular around the world and

   _____.

   a. is taken in much the same way everywhere

   b. many different tea customs have developed

   c. is considered a sacred remedy for many illnesses

2. The tea ceremony in Japan

   _____.

   a. is formal and complicated

   b. is similar to the British way of serving tea

   c. was borrowed from the Chinese

3. Regardless of the country, tea is

   _____.

   a. an important part of social life

   b. served very formally

   c. always offered to guests

B. Looking for Details

Circle T is the sentence is true. Circle F if the sentence is false.

1. Tea was first used as a medicine in China and Japan.   T   F
2. The Chinese drank their tea from bowls with lids.   T   F
3. Drinking tea never became an important part of Chinese life.   T   F
4. The Japanese tea ceremony was recently developed.   T   F
5. During the Japanese tea ceremony, guests must appear proud.   T   F
6. At the end of the tea ceremony, it is polite to make a loud sound to show how good the tea is.   T   F
7. The British only drink tea in the morning and evening.   T   F
8. The British like to serve tea in a very informal way.   T   F
9. The Koreans like to eat raw eggs during sips of tea.   T   F
10. In Morocco, a guest is expected to drink only one glass of tea.   T   F

C. Making Inferences and Drawing Conclusions

The answers to these questions are not directly stated in the passage. Write complete sentences.

1. Why do you think tea was served with so much ceremony by the ancient Chinese and Japanese?
2. Why is tea drinking an important part of British daily life?
3. Why is tea considered part of the social life in many countries?
4. Why is tea considered a remedy for body and spirit?

DISCUSSION

Discuss these questions with your classmates.

1. Compare the way Americans drink tea or coffee with the way people drink it in your country.
2. Describe polite table manners in your country as compared with the United States.
3. What is expected of a host or guest in your country?

WRITING

ORGANIZATION

Comparing and Contrasting

In the previous chapter, we looked at **block organization** of a compare and contrast essay where you discuss the similarities in one block and the differences in another. In this chapter, we will look at **point-by-point organization**. With this type of organization, the similarities and differences of the same point are discussed together. The **point-by-point organization** pattern looks like this:

Topic: The Similarities and Differences in the Food of the North and the Food of the South of China

I. Basic Ingredients

   A. Similarities: North and South

   B. Differences: North and South

II. Use of Spices

   A. Similarities: North and South

   B. Differences: North and South

III. Famous Chinese Dishes

    A. Similarities: North and South

    B. Differences: North and South

Compare this organization with the block organization on page 100. In point-by-point organization, the comparison and contrast of the points may be in any order that is appropriate for the topic. You may order the most important point first or last.

In both types of organization, you must constantly use comparison and contrast structure words to show whether your points are similar or different.

Using *Although, Even Though,* and *Though*

Although, even though and **though** all have the same meaning. They introduce an adverbial clause that shows a contrast or an unexpected idea. These clauses are useful when we are comparing and contrasting something.

Examples

    Although the tea was very special, I didn't like the taste.

    Even though the tea was very special, I didn't like the taste.

    Though the tea was very special, I didn't like the taste.

Note the use of the comma in the above sentences.

Exercise 1

Combine the two sentences into one sentence using although or even though.

1. The British are tea drinkers. Many people drink coffee.

2. In Asia, people drink tea plain. The British prefer tea with milk added.

3. Most people make tea from tea leaves. The Burmese eat tea leaves as salad.

4. In Asia and Europe, tea is usually made in a ceramic or china teapot. In Morocco, a brass or silver teapot is used.

5. Coffee has been regarded as the most popular beverage in the United States. Soft drinks are consumed twice as much.

WRITING PRACTICE

Choose one of the following topics.

1. Compare and contrast the way food is served and eaten in the United States with food customs in your country.

2. Compare and contrast behavior expected from a guest or host in your country with that in the United States.

3. Compare the experience of eating in a restaurant in your country with eating in one in the United States.

1. Pre-writing.

Work with a partner, a group, or alone.

1. Brainstorm the topic. Choose a pre-writing technique you prefer.

2. Brainstorm for similarities and differences.

3. Work on a thesis statement.

2. Outlining.

A. The next step is to organize your ideas.

Step 1: *Write your thesis statement.*

Step 2: *Choose three good points of comparison and contrast from your brainstorming activity.*

Step 3: *Remember to order each point with its similarities and differences.*

B. Make a more detailed outline. The essay outline on page 17 will help you.

3. Write a rough draft.

4. Revise your rough draft.

Using the checklist below, check your rough draft or let your partner check it.

Essay Organization

Introduction: _____ General Statements
                 _____ Thesis Statement

Body: _____ Order paragraphs by points. Then give similarities and differences for each point.
                 _____ Use of different transitions to show comparison and contrast.

Conclusion: _____ Summary of main points or a statement of your thesis in other words and a final comment on the topic.

Paragraph Organization

Topic Sentence: _____ Does each of your body paragraphs have a topic sentence with a controlling idea?

Supporting Sentences:
                 _____ Is each paragraph about one main idea? Do your sentences support your topic sentence?
                 _____ Do you have specific details or examples to support what you have stated?

5. Edit Your Essay,

Work with a partner or a teacher to edit your essay. Correct spelling, punctuation, vocabulary, and grammar. Use the following editing symbols.

- cap   Capital letter
- sp   Spelling mistake
- sv   Mistake in agreement of subject and verb
- ^   Omission (You have left something out.)
- frag   Sentence fragment (Correct by completing sentence.)
- ro   Run-on sentence (Insert period and capital letter or add comma and conjunction.)

6. Write your final copy.

INTERESTING FOOD FACTS

Work with a partner or alone to see if you can complete the following food facts. Circle the letter of the best answer.

1. There are many varieties of red peppers (which have a very high vitamin C content). In Mexico today, there are _____ varieties.

   a. fifty-four

   b. twenty-one

   c. ninety-two

2. Coleslaw is a popular American dish. The _____ first introduced this dish to the United States.

   a. British

   b. Germans

   c. Dutch

3. It is believed that pasta originally came from _____.

   a. Italy

   b. China

   c. Spain

4. The first leavened bread (bread that is not flat) originated in _____.

   a. Egypt

   b. France

   c. Greece

5. A French sailor named Frazier brought this fruit back from Chile to Europe. This plant, which adapts itself well to different climates, has a red fruit with tiny seeds outside. The fruit has a special sweet smell owing to its thirty-five different chemicals. This fruit is the _____.

   a. pineapple

   b. strawberry

   c. raspberry

6. This food originated with the nomadic Turks. It is made by adding bacteria to milk and keeping it warm for several hours. _____ has recently become popular in Europe and the United States.

    a. Cream cheese

    b. Sweet butter

    c. Yogurt

7. You have to pick a lot of flowers to get a small amount of this spice. As a result, it is the most expensive spice in the world. _____ is used as a sedative in medicine and as a yellow color for food, especially rice.

    a. Saffron

    b. Curry

    c. Yellow mustard

UNIT 6

Language

Chapter 11: Our Changing Language

American Auto Telephonics
Company
February 5, 1994

Dear Sir:

Everybody in our company is
very impressed with your latest
car phone. What businessman
(or his wife?) would want to be
without one? Please have your
salesmen phone us to arrange a
presentation.

Sincerely yours,

Mrs. Jane Johnson

Mrs. Jane Johnson
President

American Auto Telephonics
Company
February 5, 1994

Dear Sales Agent:

Everybody in our company is
very impressed with your latest
car phone. What business
professional (or business
professional's spouse) would
want to be without one? Please
have your salespeople phone us
to arrange a presentation.

Sincerely yours,

Ms. Jane Johnson

Ms. Jane Johnson
President

PRE-READING QUESTIONS

Discuss these questions with your classmates or teacher.

 1 What is the difference between these two letters?

2 What words did the writer change?

3 Which one do you think is better? Why?

Reading: Our Changing Language

Before computers were invented, the words *byte* and *modem* did not exist, and a *mouse* was something that made some people scream and run away. Words are added to language every day, but not only as new things are invented. Changes in society also cause changes in language. For example, today the people of the **former** Soviet Union use words like *free market* and *capitalism*.

Changes in **attitude** also affect language. As people become more sensitive to the rights and needs of individuals, it becomes necessary to change the words we use to describe them. The elderly are now called *senior citizens*. The handicapped are described as *physically challenged*. Many of the words we once used had negative feelings attached to them. New words show an **awareness** in today's society that differences are good and that everyone deserves respect. Even the names of certain jobs have changed so that workers can be proud of what they do. The trashman is now called a sanitation worker, a doorman is an attendant, and a janitor is a custodian.

Many of the words we use to identify people have changed many times in recent years. Sometimes it is difficult to know what is right and what is wrong. Do we call a person of color a Black or an African-American? Is it better to say Native Americans or American Indians? And whatever do we do with the Man of the Year? If we don't know what the proper words are, then we must use sensitivity, respect, and even a little imagination.

One important influence on our language in the past decade has been the changing **role** of women in modern society. There was a time when an unmarried woman was called a **spinster**. But that was before women went into space in rockets, worked underground in mines, and were managers of corporations. As women entered more and more areas that were once thought of as men's jobs, it became necessary to change the job titles. For example, a mailman is now a mail carrier, a watchman is a guard, a lineman is a line repairer. And the Man of the Year? Well, she's the Newsmaker of the Year.

These new attitudes have also helped men, and some job titles have been changed to include them. Stewardesses are now called flight attendants. A laundress is a laundry worker, and a maid is a houseworker, because men wash floors too!

Sometimes the way words have changed seems **awkward** and silly, such as using chair for chairman, fisher for fisherman, and drafter for draftsman. But change is never easy. People often fight change until it becomes a familiar part of everyday life.

Women have fought long and hard to be treated equally in language as well as in society because they know that language can cause changes in attitudes. If every person isn't **referred to** as *he*, people will begin to realize that men aren't the only ones who are important or who have made great **achievements**. Most words that indicate only one **gender** have been replaced with words that refer to both males and females. Thus a poetess is called a poet, a waitress is a server, and mankind has become humankind.

VOCABULARY

What are the meanings of the underlined words? Circle the letter of each correct answer.

1. The people of the <u>former</u> Soviet Union use words like capitalism.
    a. new
    b. changing
    c. previous

2. Changes in <u>attitude</u> also affect language.
    a. the way we feel and think
    b. the way we move
    c. the way we speak

3. New words show an <u>awareness</u> in today's society that differences are good.
    a. quickness
    b. confusion
    c. knowledge and understanding

4. One important influence on our language has been the changing <u>role</u> of women in modern society.
    a. group
    b. position
    c. looks

5. Sometimes the way words have changed seems <u>awkward</u> and silly.
    a. strange
    b. useless
    c. incorrect

6. If every person isn't <u>referred to</u> as *he*, people will realize men aren't the only ones who are important.

    a. sent as

    b. classified as

    c. thought of

7. Men aren't the only ones who are responsible for <u>achievements</u>.

    a. inventions

    b. businesses

    c. successes

8. Most words that indicate only one <u>gender</u> have been replaced with words that refer to both males and females.

    a. group

    b. word

    c. sex

COMPREHENSION

A. Looking for the Main Ideas

Circle the letter of the correct answer.

1. Words are added to language _____.

    a. only when new things are invented

    b. only when society changes

    c. all the time

2. Language is also affected by _____.

    a. changes in attitude

    b. changes with the elderly and handicapped

    c. being different

3. An important influence on our language recently has been _____.

    a. the changing role of managers

    b. the changing jobs of men

    c. the changing role of women

B. Looking for Details

Scan the passage quickly to find the answers to these questions. Write complete answers.

1. What are the changed names for trashman and doorman?
2. What was an unmarried woman called in the past?
3. What are today's job titles for a mailman and a watchman?
4. What do we say instead of Man of the Year?
5. Women used to be stewardesses, laundresses, and maids. What are these job titles today?
6. Which three words that have changed seem awkward?
7. What do we say instead of "mankind"?

C. Making Inferences and Drawing Conclusions

The answers to these questions are not directly stated in the passage. Write complete sentences.

1. Who do you think will fight some of these changes in language?
2. Are the words that have changed more accurate?

DISCUSSION

Discuss these questions with your classmates.

1. Discuss the following new ways to identify people and things. Are these good changes? Can you improve them?

Old	New
businessmen	businesspeople
salesman/woman	sales clerk
deliveryman	deliverer, delivery clerk
manpower	personnel, staff, people power
repairman	repairer
hostess	host
housewife	homemaker
motherland/fatherland	homeland
manmade	synthetic

What other words can you think of that can be changed?

2. Describe some changes in the language of your country.

Read the following essay written by a student. Underline the thesis statement and the topic sentence in each of the body paragraphs.

Learning English Is Important for Me

When I first came to the United States of America, I found out the importance of knowing English. Whenever I went to the market to buy food, to the post office to mail a letter, or to take a bus to a bank, I had to communicate in English or things would not go smoothly. But the two most important reasons for learning English for me are to be able to go through the interview process to get a job and be able to read English and know what is going on in the world.

First, learning English is essential if I wish to go through the interview process to get a job. It is important to feel comfortable with the language and be able to converse without hesitation with the interviewer. Even if the interview may be in another language, sometimes the interviewer will switch to English just to test your fluency. But conversation is not enough, I must be able to understand formal written English, including contracts. When I was in Hong Kong, I went for an interview and was given a letter of employment to read and sign. The letter stated, "You will have a nine-month probation period and one month's notice or payment in lieu of notice has to be given if either party wants to terminate the contract during the probation period." I did not know what "payment in lieu of" or "terminate" meant. I could not ask the interviewer or I would not get the job. I signed the contract, and started the job. I quit six months later without prior notice. Because I did not understand the contract, I lost a month's salary.

Second, learning English is important for me because I want to know what is going on around me in the world. When I read newspapers and magazines in my own language, I feel I am not getting enough news of the world. I believe that Western reporters communicate all kinds of news in greater detail, and this will give me a different perspective. Also, being able to read magazines and newspapers in English will keep me abreast of the technological changes that will be affecting us all. With recent advances in technology, the world is changing rapidly in many fields, such as business, arts, and medicine. These changes will affect me soon and it is important for me to read and keep up with these changes.

In conclusion, it is important for me to learn English so that I will feel confident about myself when I go for a job interview again. It is also important because I want to know what is happening in the world around me, and by learning English I can do this. In fact, learning English is the answer to a lot of the things that I need and want.

ORGANIZING

Cause and Effect

In this unit, you will look at a situation (effect) and examine the reasons or **causes** for it. Usually there is more than one reason for a situation. It is important to look at all the reasons. When there are many reasons, there is usually one that is most important.

When you write about the causes of an effect, remember the following.

1. Look at all the possible causes and discuss them.
2. Support all the causes. Give good examples.
3. State your most important cause last. This will make your essay more interesting. If you state your most important cause first, the reader will not have anything to look forward to.

Look at the student model essay. Notice these points.

   a. The thesis statement tells the reader what the situation is and that there are reasons or causes for this situation.

   b. Each of the body paragraphs gives a cause or reason and supports it with examples.

   c. Each paragraph starts with a different transition. The transitions used for chronological order can also be used to introduce a cause.

Transition for Showing Cause: *Because/As*

Because and **as** introduce a reason clause. They both answer the question "Why?" Both **because** and **as** can be used at the beginning of a sentence or in the middle.

Example

   Statement: Language is changing.
   Reason: The roles of women are changing in modern society.

                  as
   Language is changing **because** the roles of women are changing in modern society.or

   Because
   As the roles of women are changing in modern society, language is changing in modern society.

Note: Use a comma after the reason if you start the sentence with **because** or **as**.

Exercise 1

Join the sentences with* as. *Write each sentence in two ways.

   1. **As** in the middle
   2. **As** in the beginning

   1. Language changes. Society changes.

   _____

   _____

   2. Words are added to the language every day. New things are invented.

   _____

   _____

3. There is a need to change some job titles. Women are entering areas that were once thought of as men's jobs.

_____

_____

_____

WRITING PRACTICE

Choose one of the following topics.

1. As society and times change, words in English (or your language) need to change too. Give two or more reasons for this.
2. The spelling of English words needs to change. Give two or more reasons for this.
3. Learning English is important in my life. Give two or more reasons for this.

1. Pre-writing.

Work with a partner, a group, or alone.

1. Brainstorm the topic. Choose a pre-writing technique you prefer.
2. Brainstorm for reasons and ideas about each reason.
3. Work on a thesis statement.

2. Outlining.

A. The next step is to organize your ideas.

Step 1: *Write your thesis statement.*

Step 2: *Pick the two best reasons from your brainstorming activity (choose three reasons for a three-paragraph body).*

Step 3: *Remember to begin your paragraphs with different transition words for showing causes and their order of importance. Keep your most important cause last.*

B. Make a more detailed outline. The essay outline below will help you.

Cause and Effect Essay Outline

Introduction	*Thesis:* state situation and reasons for this.
Body	*Topic Sentence:* First cause or reason and supporting sentences. *Topic Sentence:* Second cause or reason and supporting sentences.
Conclusion	Restatement of your thesis and a final comment.

3. Write a rough draft.

4. Revise your rough draft.

Using the checklist below, check your rough draft or let your partner check it.

Essay Checklist

Essay Organization

Introduction: _____ General Statements
_____ Thesis Statement

Body: _____ Logical organization of reasons, with the most important reason last.
_____ Use of different transitions to show cause and order.

Conclusion: _____ Summary of main points or statement of your thesis in other words and a final comment on the topic.

Paragraph Organization

Topic Sentence: _____ Does each of your body paragraphs have a topic sentence with a controlling idea?

Supporting Sentences:
_____ Is each paragraph about one main idea? Do your sentences support your topic sentence?
_____ Do you have specific factual details to support what you have stated?

5. Edit Your Essay,

Work with a partner or a teacher to edit your essay. Correct spelling, punctuation, vocabulary, and grammar. Use the following editing symbols.

- cap   Capital letter
- sp   Spelling mistake
- sv   Mistake in agreement of subject and verb
- ^   Omission (You have left something out.)
- frag   Sentence fragment (Correct by completing sentence.)
- ro   Run-on sentence (Insert period and capital letter or add comma and conjunction.)

6. Write your final copy.

Chapter 12: English Around the World

PRE-READING QUESTIONS

Discuss these questions with your classmates or teacher.

 Describe the picture. What country do you think it is?

 In your country, what English words do you see on the streets, in shops, and in eating places?

3 Why do people like to use these English words or like American culture?

Reading: English Around the World

Do you speak English? That question is frequently asked in countries around the world. Although there are almost three thousand languages, English is the most universal. It is the official language in over forty countries and the most used language in international business, science, and medicine.

Even in countries where English is not the first language, a number of English words are used. No other language is **borrowed** from more often than English. For example, a French worker looks forward to *le weekend*. A Romanian shopper catches a ride on the *trolleybus*. A Chinese businessperson talks on the *te le fung* (telephone). Some Swedish schoolgirls have even started making the plural form of words by adding -s, as in English, instead of the Swedish way of adding *-ar*, *-or*, or *-er*.

Hundreds of words borrowed from English can now be found in other languages, words such as soda, hotel, golf, tennis, jeans, O.K., baseball, and airport. Although many words are used just as they are, others are changed to make them more like the native language and therefore easier to say and remember. Thus a Japanese workers gets stuck in *rushawa* (rush hour) traffic. A Spanish mother tells her child to put on her *sueter* (sweater), and a Ukranian man goes to the barber for a *herkot* (haircut).

English is everywhere. It is on signs, clothing, soft drinks, and household products around the world. In spite of the popularity of English words and phrases, however, they are not always welcome. Some people think that the use of English words is **threatening** the purity of their native language. In 1975, the French started a commission to try to stop, and even gave **fines** for, the use of English words. Some countries have tried to **eliminate** English as their official language in order to save their native tongue.

On the other hand, some people believe that English should be the international language. They give a number of reasons for this, such as the cost of translations and the misunderstandings that result from language differences. They believe that things would run more smoothly if everyone spoke the same language.

"What would become of our many different cultures?" others argue. "Certainly the world would be a much less interesting place," they add. Indeed, there is serious **concern** on the part of language experts that many languages are disappearing. In some parts of the world, only a few people are left who can speak their native tongue. In Ireland, for example, there are only a few small areas where people speak Gaelic, the native Irish language. One expert says that half of the world's languages are dying because children are no longer learning them.

Languages have changed and disappeared throughout history. With progress, change is **inevitable**. Some things are worth **preserving**. Others are not. The difficulty is in deciding what is worth keeping. Because people have very strong feelings about the importance of their native language, we probably will not have a universal language in the near future. What is certain, however, is that English words will continue to **pop up** everywhere, from Taiwan to Timbuktu, whether some people like it or not.

VOCABULARY

What are the meanings of the underlined words. Circle the letter of each correct answer.

1. No other language is <u>borrowed</u> from more than English.
    a. born
    b. taken
    c. developed

2. The purity of their native language is <u>threatened</u>.
    a. improved
    b. in doubt
    c. in danger

3. The French gave <u>fines</u> for the use of English.
    a. punishment by taking money
    b. points
    c. prison punishment

4. Some countries have tried to <u>eliminate</u> English as their official language as a way of saving their native tongue.
    a. remove
    b. welcome
    c. exchange

5. There is serious <u>concern</u> that many languages are disappearing.
    a. hope
    b. worry
    c. discussion

6. With progress, change is inevitable.

    a. cannot be stopped

    b. possible

    c. not possible

7. Some things are worth preserving.

    a. changing

    b. avoiding

    c. keeping

8. It is certain that English words will continue to pop up everywhere.

    a. appear

    b. die

    c. change

COMPREHENSION

A. Looking for the Main Ideas

Circle the letter of the best answer.

1. No other language _____.

    a. has more letters than English

    b. is borrowed from as often as English

    c. is official in every country as English

2. According to language experts, many languages in the world _____.

    a. are learned only by children

    b. are less interesting because they are dying

    c. are disappearing

3. In the near future, English _____.

    a. will continue to appear in other languages

    b. will be the only language in the world

    c. will have to change

B. Looking for Details

Scan the passage quickly to find the answers to these questions. Write complete answers.

1. In how many countries is English the official language?
2. What has a Swedish person borrowed from English?
3. Give examples of two English words that have been changed to make them more like the native language of the speakers.
4. What did the French do in 1975 to stop the use of English words?
5. What is Gaelic?
6. Who is saying that many of the world's languages are disappearing?

C. Making Inferences and Drawing Conclusions

The answers to these question are not directly stated in the passage. Write complete sentences.

1. Which country feels that the purity of its language is threatened by having English words in its language?
2. What is the main language spoke in Ireland?
3. What do you think will happen to Gaelic in Ireland?
4. Which languages do you think are disappearing?
5. Do you think English will be a global language one day?

DISCUSSION

Discuss these questions with your classmates.

1. Make a list of ten of the most popular English words used in your country, and write how you say them. Compare your list with that of a partner from a different country.
2. Give the names of the most popular U.S. television programs or movies you watch in your country. In which language do you watch them?
3. Name some American foods or clothes popular in your country.
4. Name some American sport or type of music popular in your country.

Cause and Effect Essay

In Chapter 10, we looked at an essay where you give reasons for something. In this chapter, we will look at how to organize an essay that gives reasons for something, and then discusses the results. This is a **cause and effect** essay.

There are two ways to organize a cause and effect essay: "block" organization and "chain" organization.

1. **Block Organization:** You discuss all of the causes in one block (one, two, or three paragraphs, depending on the number of causes). Then you discuss all the effects in another block.

2. **Chain Organization:** You discuss the cause and then its effect, a second cause and its effect, a third cause and its effect, and so on.

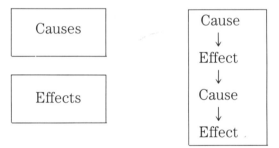

The type of organization you choose for your cause and effect essay will depend on your topic. Some topics work better when organized in a block, while others work better when organized in a chain. If the causes and effects are closely related, it is better to use a chain organization.

Cause and Effect Structure Words

These words and phrases signal a cause or an effect. Here are some that you may already know.

Cause Structure Words	Effect Structure Words
The first reason . . .	The first effect . . .
The next cause . . .	As a result, . . .
Because of . . .	Consequently, . . .

The cause structure words signal a reason for something.

Example:

Children are no longer learning the native tongues of their grandfathers. (reason)

The effect structure words signal the result.

Example:

Many languages are disappearing. (effect)

Which Are the Causes?
Which Are the Effects?

It is important to understand the difference between the cause and the effect. Remember that an effect can have several causes.

Example:

Today the Japanese use many English words. **(effect)**
The Japanese watch American TV programs. **(cause)**
The Japanese listen to American pop music. **(cause)**

Exercise 1

Identify which is the cause and which is the effect.

_____ 1. Half of the world's languages are dying.
_____   Children no longer learn them.

_____ 2. The Umutina tribal language of South America disappeared.
_____   The only person who spoke the language died in 1988.

_____ 3. Children in France are not learning the Breton language in schools.
_____   The Breton language in France is near extinction.

_____ 4. The Amish, a religious group in America, have kept their language, Pennsylvania Dutch, alive for three centuries.
_____   They speak Pennsylvania Dutch at home.
_____   They do not have telephones or television.

Therefore and *Consequently*

Therefore and **consequently** are sentence connectors. They connect two clauses when the second clause is the result of the first clause. **Consequently** and **therefore** have the same meaning as the coordinator **so**.

Example:

English is the most universal language. **(statement)**
It is the language most used for science, medicine, and business.
(result)

                 ; consequently,
English is the most universal language; **therefore**, it is the language most used for science, medicine, and business.

Note: Use a semicolon before and a comma after **consequently** and **therefore**.

Exercise 2

Read the pairs of sentences. Choose the clause that gives the result. Then combine the sentences, adding **therefore** *or* **consequently** *before the result clause. Punctuate the sentences.*

1. Sometimes English words are changed to make them more like the native language.

   They are easier to say and remember.

   _____

   _____

2. In France, where English is not spoken, many words are borrowed.

   A French worker looks forward to *le weekend*.

   _____

   _____

3. English words are becoming popular in other languages. Some people are afraid that the purity of their language is threatened.

_____

_____

4. There will be no universal language in the near future. People have strong feelings about the importance of their language.

_____

_____

WRITING PRACTICE

Choose one of the following topics.

1. The causes and effects of having English as a global language.
2. The effects English (American music, food, sports, etc.) has had on your language and culture.
3. What effects have the English language and culture had on you?

1. Pre-writing.

Work with a partner, a group, or alone.

1. Brainstorm the topic. Choose a pre-writing technique that you prefer. Divide your paper into two columns. List the causes on one side and the effects on the other.
2. Brainstorm for ideas for each cause and effect.
3. Work on a thesis statement.

2. Outlining.

A. The next step is to organize your ideas.

Step 1: *Write your thesis statement.*

Step 2: *Pick the two best causes and effects from your brainstorming activity.*

Step 3: *Remember to use a variety of cause and effect structure words and connectors.*

B. Make a more detailed outlined. The essay outline below will help you.

Cause and Effect Essay Outline

Introduction	*Thesis:* state situation and reasons for this.
Body	*Topic Sentence:* First cause or reason and supporting sentences.
	Topic Sentence: Second cause or reason and supporting sentences.
Conclusion	Restatement of your thesis and a final comment.

3. Write a rough draft.

4. Revise your rough draft.

Using the checklist below, check your rough draft or let your partner check it.

Essay Checklist

Essay Organization

Introduction:　　　_____ General Statements

　　　　　　　　　_____ Thesis Statement

Body:　　　　　　　_____ Logical organization of causes and effects.

　　　　　　　　　_____ Use of cause and effect structure words.

Conclusion:　　　_____ Summary of main points or statement of your thesis in other words and a final comment on the topic.

Paragraph Organization

Topic Sentences:　_____ Does each of your body paragraphs have a topic sentence with a controlling idea?

Supporting Sentences:

　　　　　　　　　_____ Is each paragraph about one main idea? Do your sentences support your topic sentence?

　　　　　　　　　_____ Do you have specific details to support what you have stated?

5. Edit Your Essay,

Work with a partner or a teacher to edit your essay. Correct spelling, punctuation, vocabulary, and grammar. Use the following editing symbols.

- cap   Capital letter
- sp   Spelling mistake
- sv   Mistake in agreement of subject and verb
- ^   Omission (You have left something out.)
- frag   Sentence fragment (Correct by completing sentence.)
- ro   Run-on sentence (Insert period and capital letter or add comma and conjunction.)

6. Write your final copy.

FACTS ABOUT LANGUAGE

Work with a partner or alone to see if you can answer these questions.

1. How many words (not including technical terms) does the English language contain?

   a. 300,000   b. 490,000   c. 600,000

2. English is full of words "borrowed" from other languages. Which languages do you think these words came from?

   boss   karate   robot

   disco   shampoo   ketchup

   a. Chinese _____

   b. French _____

   c. Dutch _____

   d. Japanese _____

   e. Czech _____

   f. Indian _____

   Do you know any others?

3. Which language is spoken by the greatest number of people in the world?

   a. Spanish   b. Chinese   c. English

4. How many alphabets are used in the world?

    a. Ten   b. Twenty-six   c. Sixty-five

5. What is Ameslan?

    a. A language spoken by the Dutch

    b. A language spoken in Papua New Guinea

    c. American Sign Language

UNIT 7

Technology

Chapter 13: What's So Good About the Information Age?

PRE-READING QUESTIONS

Discuss these questions with your classmates or teacher.

1 What is the purpose of the machine this man is using?

2 Would you like to have one of these machines?

3 What would you use it for?

Reading: What's So Good About the Information Age?

Shop for new shoes. Buy groceries. Stop by library and look up *N.Y. Times* article for work. Pick up this week's *People* magazine at newsstand. Go to video store and rent movie for tonight. See travel agent about plane tickets to Denver. Stop by box office and pick up tickets for baseball game. Call Mom.

If your daily "List of Things to Do" makes your head spin, then you'll be happy to know that relief is in sight. In the near future, time will be on your side when the "information highway" runs directly through your home and makes **running errands** almost **obsolete**.

How is this possible? By combining the technologies of computers, telephones, and television and then finding new methods of storing and **transmitting** data, an "electronic superhighway" will transport an **infinite** amount of information to every home. Videophones will allow users to see the person they are calling and to receive information such as a train schedule, a list of local shoe stores, or even an article from yesterday's newspaper.

Home computers **plugged into** phone lines will become powerful tools of knowledge because they will be connected to libraries, universities, and major research **facilities**. A doctor will have easy **access** to information about a rare disease. An engineer will be able to locate the latest facts on how to make a building earthquake safe. Parents will have the opportunity to learn about child care. A home gardener will find out how to plant a new rose bush. From the **vitally** important to the most common, the "superhighway" will carry it all.

Computerized, or "smart," TVs and new satellite systems will change the face of television as we know it. Instead of a handful of programs, as many as 550 channels will be available. Home shopping programs will allow viewers to shop for everything from a boat to a loaf of bread. Travel services, weather reports, video games, financial services, art courses, and French lessons will all be available at the touch of a button.

An astonishing variety of programming will be offered—more news, documentaries, and educational programs, as well as sports, old and new television shows, and movies. The TV guide will be the size of a telephone book! Well, not really, because that will be on television too. People will look at the list and make their selections, from an old movie like *Casablanca* to a newly released action film, or they might choose a service such as shopping, vacation planning, banking, or bill paying. The possibilities are almost endless.

This new technology will be the greatest invention since the **printing press**. Just as the printing press made books available to the **masses**, the "superhighway" will open up a whole new world of knowledge to the public. If someone wants to know how to fix a leaky pipe, cook a chicken, invest money, or paint a watercolor picture, the answers to those questions, as well as information on an infinite variety of other subjects, will be available to viewers right in their homes.

Meanwhile, the time saved by not having to travel from one place to another for information, goods, and services will be available for rest, recreation, and education. When the "superhighway" is running, it will greatly improve the quality of life. The world will certainly become a more interesting, if not a much better, place in which to live.

VOCABULARY

Complete the definitions with one of the following words.

running errands	plugged into	printing press
obsolete	facilities	masses
transmitting	access	
infinite	vitally	

1. The machine that puts words on paper for newspapers and books

   is the _____.

2. You are _____ if you are

   going from place to place taking care of things that need to be

   done.

3. All people make up the

   _____.

4. Something that is no longer useful is

   _____.

5. Sending things, like messages, from one person or place to

   another is _____.

6. Something _____ is so great

   or numerous it seems to be without end.

7. Something _____ important

is of the greatest necessity.

8. We have _____ to things if

we can get to them and use them.

9. _____ are built and

established for a particular purpose, such as training and

education.

10. When an electrical piece of equipment is connected to an

electrical power point, it is

_____.

COMPREHENSION

A. Looking for the Main Ideas

Circle the letter of the correct answer.

1. The "electronic superhighway" will

_____.

a. not affect the general population

b. carry an infinite variety of information

c. be useful only to libraries and universities

2. The most important advantage of the "electronic superhighway"
is that _____.

a. people will get more news programs

b. people will learn how to invest money

c. people will have the greater access to information

3. "Smart" TVs _____.

a. will require a TV guide the size of a telephone book

b. will educate instead of entertain

c. will offer an amazing choice of programs

B. Looking for Details

Complete the following sentences.

1. The "electronic superhighway" will combine the technologies of

   _____.

2. The "electronic superhighway" will transmit

   _____ to each and every

   home in the nation.

3. Videophones will allow users to

   _____

   and _____.

4. By plugging home computers into phone lines, users will have

   access to _____.

5. The kind of information the "superhighway" will carry

   is _____.

6. The word "smart" TV means the television

   is _____.

7. "Smart" TVs will offer viewers

   _____.

8. The technology of the information "superhighway" can be

   compared to the invention of the printing press because

   _____.

9. The information "superhighway" is expected to save a lot of time

   for people because _____.

10. Some people believe that the time saved by the information

    "superhighway" will be available for

    _____.

C. Making Inferences and Drawing Conclusions

The answers to these questions are not directly stated in the passage. Write complete sentences.

1. Why will the "electronic superhighway" improve people's lives?
2. Why will home computers become powerful tools of knowledge?
3. How will the quality of television viewing improve?

DISCUSSION

Discuss these questions with your classmates.

1. Do you think the information highway will bring people together or isolate them?
2. Do you think that the time saved by the information highway will be used to improve the quality of life?
3. Do you think there are advantages of having 550 TV channels?

WRITING

Read the following essay written by a student. Underline the thesis statement and the topic sentence in each of the body paragraphs.

Against Advanced Technology

We are now living in the twentieth century in which various kinds of technology have been developed and are being developed. Some examples of these are computers, videotelephones, computerized television, and satellite systems. People have benefited and are benefiting from these kinds of technology, but there negative sides to them also. I do not support the idea of having a new information age because it encourages people not to read and think, and it also makes it easy for others to get personal information about you.

The first reason against the new technology is that it takes time away from reading and thinking. Before television, people used to read, think, and converse. They had the time to look at their lives and values. Today, people prefer to watch exciting things on video and television. Few people find time to read books, journals, and newspapers. Students today belong to the "TV generation" and find it hard to read a book. This affects their ability to study for school. Also, because people do not read or think, they cannot look at their own lives and values.

Secondly, because most services are or will be computerized, it is easy for others to get information about a person. For example, right now if you give a check to someone, your bank account number will be on it, and if someone finds out your Social Security number, it will be easy for that person to know how much money you have in your bank account. Also, the use of a credit card number to pay your bills or go shopping can take away your privacy. Someone can easily find out what you bought and what you paid for it. This can also lead to others using your credit card number, or, in other words, theft.

In conclusion, we have a very comfortable life because of modern technology, but it has created some negative aspects such as taking time away from reading and meditating, and it is also taking away our privacy. It is important to develop modern technology, but I think it is also important to realize and solve its negative aspects.

ORGANIZING

Writing an Argument Essay

When you write an argument or persuasion essay, you give reasons to support your ideas for or against something. When writing your essay, you may use description, comparison and contrast, or cause and effect to illustrate your points.

First, find relevant reasons to support your argument. Your reasons may be facts or opinions. Then develop your reasons into paragraphs using relevant facts, examples, and opinions. You may use the following transitions to begin your body paragraphs:

The first reason . . .
The second reason . . .
In addition, . . .

When listing the points to support your argument, some may be **facts** and some may be **opinions**. Facts are statements that are known to be true. Opinions are personal beliefs that may or may not be true. You may use both facts and opinions in an argument essay. However, if you use only opinions, your argument may not be so convincing. It is, therefore, important to distinguish between fact and opinion.

Example:

Fact: In 1985, Americans owned 137,300,000 passenger vehicles.
Opinion: Computers are taking jobs away from people.

Exercise 1

Which of the following statements are facts and which are opinions?
Write F for Fact and O for opinion.

_____ 1. Remote villages need to be in touch with the rest of the world.

_____ 2. Job stress in the United States has more than doubled since 1980.

_____ 3. Wages in the Carolinas and Tennessee are 13% to 23% lower than those in California.

_____ 4. High tech does not deliver the results it promises.

_____ 5. The multimedia "smart" TVs will become popular because of their novelty.

_____ 6. Computer-aided design (CAD) matches color, simulates texture, and gives a 3-D presentation.

_____ 7. Because of computer-aided design, today's fashions are much more creative.

_____ 8. With the "electronic superhighway," office jobs will no longer be needed.

Relevant or Not Relevant

It is also important that the statements in support of your argument be relevant or be directly connected to the argument.

Exercise 2

Work in groups or alone and decide which of the following statements
are relevant to the argument given below.

Argument: Callers prefer to get a computer instead of a human telephone operator.

_____ 1. Telephone companies are saving money by laying off operators.

_____ 2. In a survey conducted in Atlanta, 60% of the callers surveyed preferred the computerized voice on the phone.

_____ 3. Callers find that they can complete their calls much faster when using the electronic operator.

_____ 4. The telephone companies using electronic operators are not reducing calling rates.

_____ 5. A human operator may not always have a pleasant voice or tone.

After giving reasons with relevant and specific details to support your argument, you can conclude with one of the following:

In conclusion, . . .
Finally, . . .
Thus, . . .
For these reasons, . . .
As a result, . . .

WRITING PRACTICE

Choose one of the following topics.

1. Write an argument in favor of or against having a "smart" TV.
2. Write an argument in favor of or against having 550 channels to watch on TV.
3. Write an argument in favor of or against working from home using the "electronic superhighway."

1. Pre-writing.

Work with a partner, a group, or alone.

1. Brainstorm the topic. Choose a pre-writing technique you prefer.
2. Brainstorm for reasons either for or against the argument. Brainstorm for possible supporting details for each reason.
3. Work on a thesis statement.

2. Outlining.

A. The next step is to organize your ideas.

Step 1: *Write your thesis statement.*

Step 2: *Pick the two best reasons in favor of or against the argument from your brainstorming activity.*

Step 3: *Remember to begin your paragraphs with different transition words for giving reasons.*

B. Make a more detailed outline. The essay outline on page 17 will help you.

3. Write a rough draft.

4. Revise your rough draft.

Using the checklist below, check your rough draft or let your partner check it.

Essay Checklist

Essay Organization

Introduction: _____ General Statements

_____ Thesis Statement

Body: _____ Give relevant reasons for your argument. Write a paragraph for each reason. Remember to identify your reasons as opinion or fact.

_____ Use different transitions to show reasons and order.

Conclusion: _____ Summary of main points or a statement of your thesis in other words and a final comment on the topic.

Paragraph Organization

Topic Sentence: _____ Does each of your body paragraphs have a topic sentence with a controlling idea?

Supporting Sentences:

_____ Is each paragraph about one main idea? Do your sentences support your topic sentence?

_____ Do you have specific factual details to support what you have stated?

5. Edit Your Essay.

Work with a partner or a teacher to edit your essay. Correct spelling, punctuation, vocabulary, and grammar. Use the following editing symbols.

- cap   Capital letter
- sp   Spelling mistake
- sv   Mistake in agreement of subject and verb
- ^   Omission (You have left something out.)
- frag   Sentence fragment (Correct by completing sentence.)
- ro   Run-on sentence (Insert period and capital letter or add comma and conjunction.)

6. Write your final copy.

Chapter 14: The Global Telephone

PRE-READING QUESTIONS

Discuss these questions with your classmates or teacher.

1 Describe the situation that the person is in.

2 How do you think the person could get out of this situation?

3 How could a telephone help this person right now?

Reading: The Global Telephone

Off you went in the Land Rover at five o'clock this morning, traveling over deeply **rutted** roads, crossing the plains that **swept** against the mountains. As far as your eyes could see, the land was flat and open, with only the umbrella-shaped trees for **adornment**. Herds of animals— zebra, elephant, giraffe, and gazelle—passed like shadows in the bright sunlight. All day you traveled until finally arriving at the camp by the Tana River near Garissa, Kenya. You set up your tents by lamplight, the mist finally cleared, and the stars looked close enough to touch. The experience was so marvelous that you had to share it with your best friend, so as you sat by the fire, you pulled a small boxlike object out of your knapsack. After extending the aerial, you called your brother, who at that moment was studying at home in New Jersey.

This may sound **far-fetched**, but soon everyone will be able to do it. Before long, the satellite phone, also known as the global telephone, will be universally available. Connected by a system of satellites circling the globe, the satellite phone will take us one giant step further than the present-day mobile phone.

To say the least, the telephone has "come a long way, baby." Once a **cumbersome** machine with wires and a big round dial, today's mobile phone consists of a tiny **panel** of buttons that fits into the palm of one's hand. It can go anywhere the hand can go—in the car, on a motorcycle, into a restaurant, on the beach, up a mountain, or into the bush. Soon mobile satellite telephones will allow us to make calls anywhere on earth.

Global telephones are a marvelous invention because they have the **potential** to bring even the most **remote** villages into touch with the rest of the world. People in places where telephone wires don't exist or are in bad repair will no longer be isolated.

Global phones could also play a part in improving a nation's economy. As remarkable as it may seem, half of the world's population now lives more than two hours away from a telephone. But with a satellite telephone, small-business owners could market their products and take orders over the phone. Farmers could ask for help in **harvesting** their crops before a **devastating** storm. A doctor could be called to help a sick child. Books could be ordered from faraway stores and libraries. Citizens could have the chance to become better educated and informed.

Another advantage of the mobile telephone is its usefulness in helping people in trouble. For example, motorists **stranded** on the highway could use mobile phones to call for help from their cars. Even adventurers in trouble on the side of a mountain or in a faraway rain forest will have rescuers at their fingertips if they carry a mobile phone.

Wherever people go, they will be able to stay in touch with friends and family and to conduct business. Parents can make sure their children are safe. Workers can stay in contact with their bosses. Police officers and emergency medical teams can call for extra help and equipment. Small-business owners, such as plumbers and builders, can take customers' calls right on their job sites. Thanks to the global telephone, new opportunities for safety, success, and advancement will soon open up for users in the Information Age.

VOCABULARY

Complete the definitions with one of the following words.

panel	cumbersome	far-fetched
stranded	rutted	dcvastating
adornment	potential	swept
harvesting	remote	

1. Something that does not seem possible is said to be

   _____.

2. An object used for _____

   would decorate and make something beautiful.

3. A _____ event would cause

   great harm and destruction.

4. A _____ is a board on which

   you can control a telephone or other kinds of instruments.

5. Something or someone with _____

   has future possibilities.

6. Something far away in space and time is

   _____.

7. To be _____ is to be left in a

   strange or difficult place without the ability to leave.

8. Something is _____ if it is

heavy and hard to carry or handle.

9. Cutting and bringing in the crops when they are ready to be used

is called _____.

10. A road with tracks caused by rain or passing vehicles is

_____.

11. Something _____ across the

sky would extend in a wide curve or range.

COMPREHENSION

A. Looking for the Main Ideas

Circle the letter of the correct answer.

1. The satellite telephone

_____.

   a. will be available to a limited number of people

   b. is an unrealistic dream for the future

   c. will bring remote villages into touch with the world
   community

2. The advantages of a mobile telephone are:

_____.

   a. it's a cumbersome machine with wires

   b. it's connected by a system of satellites

   c. it's small, lightweight, and portable

3. Satellite telephones _____.

   a. could be of great advantage to poor nations

   b. are most important for farmers and other workers

   c. will have a limited use outside the Western countries

B. Looking for Details

Complete the following sentences.

1. The global telephone does not have

   _____ and instead is

   connected to _____.

2. The global phone will take us one step further than the

   _____.

3. The global phone could help the citizens of developing countries

   to _____.

4. Global phones can help people in trouble because

   _____.

5. Global phones are very useful to businesspeople because

   _____.

6. No matter where we are in the world, the global phone will allow

   us to _____.

7. Thanks to the global telephone, new opportunities for

   _____ will soon open up for

   users.

8. Small business owners, such as plumbers and builders, can

   _____.

C. Making Inferences and Drawing Conclusions

The answers to these questions are not directly stated in the passage. write complete sentences.

1. How does the satellite phone take us one step further than our present-day mobile phone?
2. Why are global telephones a useful invention for poor nations?

3. Why might a self-employed plumber find a mobile telephone useful?

Discuss these questions with your classmates.

1. What could the disadvantages be of the global telephone?
2. Would you like to have a global telephone? If so, why?
3. Global telephones will bring people who live in remote areas into touch with the rest of the world. Do you think this is a good idea?

WRITING

ORGANIZING

Using Examples to Support Your Opinion

It is important to support your opinions with factual details. The more concrete your facts are, the more convincing your argument will be.

Look at the following examples:

Fact with lack of support	:	Most Americans have telephones.
Concrete supporting detail	:	According to the Federal Communications Commission, there were fifty-eight telephones per one hundred people in the United States, making an average of 1.6 telephones per household in 1986.
Fact with lack of support	:	The home computer is becoming popular in the United States.
Concrete supporting detail	:	In 1985, according to polls by both the Roper Organization and *USA Today*, 12% of American households owned a computer.

In the above examples, the facts are given by the Federal Communications Commission and based on polls by the Roper Organization and *USA Today*. These are the **authority**. The authority should be identified by name. Vague references to authority are not acceptable in an argument. Do not use such phrases as, "They say . . ." or "People say . . ." or "Authorities agree . . ." Make the authority a reliable source. Do not use a relative or a friend as authority. Look at the following and indicate which are reliable and concrete sources.

Exercise 1

Check the numbers of the reliable sources.

1. They say that Americans are addicted to electronics.
2. People say that, on average, they spend less than an hour traveling to and from work.
3. In 1985, the most popular activities for children who used home computers were games and educational programs, said *USA Today*.
4. Everybody knows that high tech jobs are growing at a faster than average rate.
5. According to the Recording Industry Association of America, in 1986, sales of compact disc players rose by 290%.

Remember to introduce your examples with **for example, for instance,** or **e.g.** (from Latin *exempli gratia*, for example).

WRITING PRACTICE

Choose one of the following topics.

1. Write an argument in favor of or against having the global phone.
2. Write an argument in favor of or against bringing remote villages and areas of the world into touch with the rest of the world.
3. Write an argument in favor of or against having a videophone (on which you see the person you are calling).

1. Pre-writing.

Work with a partner, a group, or alone.

1. Brainstorm the topic. Choose a pre-writing technique you prefer.
2. Brainstorm for reasons either for or against the argument. Brainstorm for possible supporting details for each reason.
3. Work on a thesis statement.

2. Outlining.

A. The next step is to organize your ideas.

Step 1: *Write your thesis statement.*

Step 2: *Pick the two best reasons in favor of or against the argument from your brainstorming activity.*

Step 3: *Remember to begin your paragraphs with different transition words for giving reasons.*

B. Make a more detailed outline. The essay outline on page 17 will help you.

3. Write a rough draft.

4. Revise your rough draft.

Using the checklist below, check your rough draft or let your partner check it.

Essay Checklist

Essay Organization

Introduction: _____ General Statements

_____ Thesis Statement

Body: _____ Give relevant reasons for your argument. Write a paragraph for each reason. Remember to identify your reasons as opinion or fact.

_____ Use different transitions to show reasons and order.

Conclusion: _____ Summary of main points or statement of your thesis in other words and a final comment on the topic.

Paragraph Organization

Topic Sentence: _____ Does each of your body paragraphs have a topic sentence with a controlling idea?

Supporting Sentences:

_____ Is each paragraph about one main idea? Do your sentences support your topic sentence?

_____ Do you have specific factual details to support what you have stated?

5. Edit Your Essay,

Work with a partner or a teacher to edit your essay. Correct spelling, punctuation, vocabulary, and grammar. Use the following editing symbols.

- cap   Capital letter
- sp   Spelling mistake
- sv   Mistake in agreement of subject and verb
- ^   Omission (You have left something out.)
- frag   Sentence fragment (Correct by completing sentence.)
- ro   Run-on sentence (Insert period and capital letter or add comma and conjunction.)

6. Write your final copy.

*Do you know the answers to these questions? Circle the letter of the
correct answer.*

1. Over a hundred years ago, an American scientist invented a
   chemical by accident. This chemical was an artificial sweetener.
   Today, people who are on a diet use it instead of sugar. What is it
   called?

   a. sucrose

   b. saccharin

   c. Nutra-sweet

2. Wolfgang Dabisch, a German, invented a new substance made in
   Frankfurt today. It's a small piece of paper coated with a white
   substance on one side. It is used when you make a typing error.
   What is the name of the invention?

   a. Tipper

   b. Type-out

   c. Tippex

3. In 1918, a machine was invented with which a ship could send
   out a sound under water. This was used to find enemy
   submarines. Today, fishing boats use it to find fish. What is the
   name of this invention?

   a. radar

   b. radioactivity

   c. sonar

4. A chemical used to kill insects was discovered in 1942. This
   insecticide was used widely but scientists later realized that it
   was dangerous for humans. What is the name of this insecticide?

   a. DDT

   b. Agent Orange

   c. ozone

5. The laser was invented by Dr. Theobald Maiman, an American scientist. Maiman made a machine that produced a much brighter light than ever before. When did he invent this machine?

    a. 1945

    b. 1970

    c. 1960

6. In 1956, the Nobel Prize was given for an invention that changed radios, TVs, and record players. The new electrical product was smaller, stronger, worked on batteries, and was portable. What was this invention?

    a. the microchip

    b. the transistor

    c. robotics

Editing Symbols

Symbol	Explanation
vt	Incorrect verb tense
vf	Verb incorrectly formed
modal	Incorrect use or formation of modal
cond	Incorrect use or formation of a conditional sentence
ss	Incorrect sentence structure
wo	incorrect or awkward word order
conn	Incorrect or missing connector
pass	Incorrect formation or use of passive voice
unclear	Unclear message
art	Incorrect or missing article
num	Problem with the singular or plural of a noun
wc	Wrong word choice, including prepositions
wf	Wrong word form
nonidiom	Nonidiomatic (not expressed this way in English)
coh	Coherence—one idea does not lead to the next
lc	Lowercase—word(s) incorrectly capitalized
p	Punctuation—punctuation incorrect or missing
pro re	Pronoun reference—pronoun reference unclear or incorrect
pro agree	Pronoun agreement—pronoun agreement unclear or incorrect
¶	Begin a new paragraph here, indent.

Brainstorming Techniques

Before writing an essay on a specific topic, we have to get ideas. This stage in prewriting is called *brainstorming*. When we brainstorm, we try and get as many ideas about a specific subject as we can. This helps us get started more quickly and saves time later in the writing process.

There are three useful brainstorming techniques:

1. listing
2. clustering
3. free writing

After you learn about each technique, decide which technique is the best one for you.

1. Listing

With the listing technique, you think about your topic and quickly make a list of all the words and phrases that come into your head. The idea is to get as many ideas as possible in a short time. Follow these steps:

1. Write down the topic at the top of your paper.
2. Make a list of all the words and phrases that come into your head about the topic. Don't stop to think if they are right or wrong or grammatically correct or incorrect. Even if you write down information not connected to the topic, you can always cross it out later.
3. Use words, phrases, and sentences.

The following is an example of the listing technique on the topic of supersitions.

Example:

Superstitions

unlucky 13	broken mirror
horse shoe	salt
honeymoon	walking under a ladder
seventh child	sneezing to the left
7—lucky number	the weather
a red sky	New Year's Day
Friday, the 13th	Christmas superstitions
Number 4—unlucky	opening an umbrella in the
lucky & unlucky numbers.	house
wedding day superstitions	lucky or unlucky objects

4. Rewrite your list putting the same ideas together. Cross out ideas that are the same or do not fit.

unlucky 13	broken mirror
horse shoe	salt
~~honeymoon~~	walking under a ladder
~~seventh child~~	~~sneezing to the left~~
7—lucky number	~~the weather~~
~~a red sky~~	~~New Year's Day~~
Friday, the 13th	~~Christmas superstitions~~
Number 4—unlucky	opening an umbrella in the house
lucky & unlucky numbers.	
~~wedding day superstitions~~	lucky or unlucky objects

From this new list "lucky or unlucky numbers" and "lucky or unlucky objects" have the most ideas. The writer can choose either of these as the focus of a paragraph.

2. Clustering

With the clustering technique, you write your topic in the center of your paper and circle it. Then you write whatever idea you get in circles around the center. Think about each idea and make more circles around it. Your best ideas will have many circles around them.

The following is an example of the clustering technique used to describe a person's character traits.

Example:

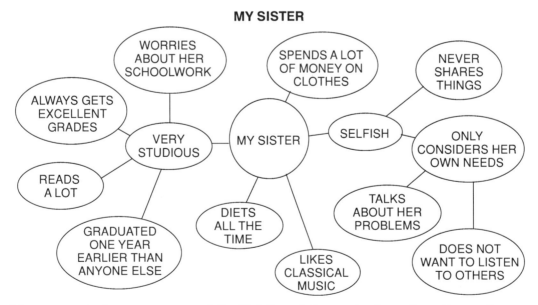

MY SISTER

The most circles were around "selfish" and "very studious," so the writer can choose either of these as the focus of a paragraph.

3. Freewriting

With the freewriting technique, you write freely about a topic until you come up with a specific focus. As you are writing one idea will lead to another. You keep on writing to generate as many ideas as you can about the topic.

Follow these steps:

1. Write the topic at the top of your paper.
2. Write as much as you can about the topic. Do not worry about grammar, spelling, organization, or relevance.
3. Write until you have run out of ideas.
4. Read your freewriting and underline the main idea(s).
5. Take the main idea and freewrite on the main idea this time.

The following is an example of the freewriting technique used to describe the effects of pollution on the environment.

The Effects of Pollution on the Environment

There are so many effects of pollution on the environment that I really don't know where to begin. Every day we hear something or other on the news. I remember last week I heard about some California beaches which were considered dangerous for swimming. It's not only bad for people but its bad for the animals too. Many birds and fish are dying because of polluted water. Many fish are dying in the sea, others are getting contaminated. Fishermen catch contaminated fish which may be sold in markets and we may get sick from eating them. Lakes and rivers are getting polluted too. Yes, and another problem is that our forests are dying. Many of the forests not only in North America but in Europe too are dying from acid rain. This in turn is affecting the balance of nature.

The writer has underlined two main ideas "Many birds and fish are dying because of polluted water." and "our forests are dying." The writer can take one of these main ideas and brainstorm by freewriting on one of the main ideas this time.

Exercise on Brainstorming Techniques

Work in a group or alone. Use one or more of the brainstorming techniques on the following topics:

1. The positive effects of television.
2. Problems of living in a big city.
3. Why learning English is important.